CONTEMPORARY BLACK LEADERS

Contemporary Black Leaders

Elton C. Fax

ILLUSTRATED WITH PHOTOGRAPHS

DODD, MEAD & COMPANY
NEW YORK

ISBN 0-396-06231-8
Library of Congress Catalog Card Number: 79-134322

Printed in the United States of America
by The Cornwall Press, Inc., Cornwall, N. Y.

3-27-73

*To the memory of my father, who in his brief life
would settle for nothing less than being a complete man*

ACKNOWLEDGMENTS

I wish to extend my sincere thanks to the following people who helped me get this book together. Lindsay Patterson for the suggestions and encouragement that initiated the project; the fourteen persons I have written about, as well as their staffs and associates—particularly William Simms and Allen Davis of The National Urban League, and Carlton Hatcher, James Taylor, Vera Hemmingway, and Charlotte Johnson of Gary, Indiana; The personnel of The Schomburg Collection of The New York Public Library, especially Ernest Kaiser and Cora Eubanks; Melvin Tapley for pictorial assistance; Anne Judge, Frances Manning, Florence Bailey, and Mattie Hubbard for making books and periodicals available to me; George S. Schuyler for important information used in the section on Roy Wilkins; Joan Bacchus for her critical reading of the manuscript; Allen Klots, Jr. for those rare qualities that make him so understanding an editor. And a special note of thanks goes to my faithful partner and assistant, Betty, who not only bravely endured me as I gathered and assembled this material, but who exhibited a loving patience as she read and typed the final draft.

ELTON C. FAX

New York City

Introduction

It is white America that has, in the main, decided who this nation's black leaders shall be. Not only has white America, itself, designated the black leaders, it has also classified them. According to the classification one is either a "moderate" leader or a "militant" leader. If one is moderate he is said to be "responsible" and therefore acceptable. If one is militant he is said to be "irresponsible" and he bears close watching. For white America it is all just that simple. There are no shadings, no variations between the two extremes. Those who believe that are in error. Not only are there subtle gradations between "moderate" and "militant," there are also shadings within each.

Militant black leaders, it is assumed, are those who say and do things that disturb and alarm white Americans. They remind America of the national stain of slavery and of its present festering heir, racism.

Black militants are generally envisioned as young. They are characterized as brash, boisterous, and exhibitionistic. Any young black American wearing an Afro hair style, a beard, dark glasses, and African style clothing is often (and erroneously) called a "black militant." If he talks loudly and persistently, many white people will think he is a "militant black leader." Many don't even bother to find out if what he is saying indicates that he has leadership qualities.

Black militant leaders, it is supposed, hold a deadly monopoly on blunt directness and an inability to compromise. Malcolm X is still considered by many Americans to have been the arch-apostle of national discord, the revelations of his astounding autobiography notwithstanding. For years he was white America's number one black militant. Currently Stokely Carmichael, Rap Brown, LeRoi Jones, James Foreman, Eldridge Cleaver, Huey Newton, and Bobby Seale collectively hold that title. Malcolm, it seems, was quite a man! To a lesser degree, Julian Bond, Dick Gregory, Fannie Lou Hamer, Richard G. Hatcher, and Floyd McKissick are also regarded as militant black leaders. But the simple fact is that any black American who speaks out forthrightly and forcefully against racial injustice upsets many white Americans. The latter simply cannot understand what the former are all about.

And "moderate" black leaders? On the surface they seem to be more accommodating to whites. They are, by and large, older than the militants. Their methods put white people less on the defensive, for their subtler approach and less strident tones are easier to take. Roy Wilkins, Senator Edward W. Brooke, Bayard Rustin, Justice Thurgood Marshall, and (now) the Late Martin Luther King represent the apex of black moderation. Whitney Young, Jr., Carl B. Stokes, and Charles Evers represent yet another moderate level.

Coming behind the militants the moderates appear to be less formidable and easier to deal with. But are they? Not necessarily. On the one hand the unbridled lawless acts of a violent "militant" minority invite whites to expose their raw, brutal capacity to put down such lawlessness. And the forces of law and order are commended by a grateful public for their prompt and firm action. But the same public reacts quite differently indeed when moderate and peaceful demands for justice are brutally resisted or coldly ignored—as they too often are. Few human beings anywhere find it easy to praise and condone naked injustice and hypocrisy especially when it is known by others that they have had some part in it. Moderate black leaders and their methods are not therefore, the push-overs they seem to be.

There is yet another equally basic fact to consider here. Both so-called moderate and militant black voices carry basically the same warnings and demands, for *both are dissatisfied with things as they are.* Both want change. So under the closest and most understanding inspection the labels "militant" and "moderate" become practically meaningless.

True, the two do not always consciously work together to bring change about, though they often do. Like all other humans they disagree and they squabble—privately and publicly. And they are encouraged to and often applauded by some whites for publicly staging their verbal battles. It is on such occasions that America and the world at large are led to believe that black Americans are not in accord in wanting their full measure of justice. Indeed some outsiders have chosen to believe that black Americans don't know *what* they want and that the majority of them are quite content with what exists. Ha! As Floyd McKissick has said over and over, "There isn't *five minutes' difference* among black leaders on the basic issues of whether we want to be part citizens or full citizens in this country we help to build. Our methods of trying to achieve full citizenship differ—but that's all!"

So this book is written to show the capacity of black leaders to agree and to differ even as they seek common goals. Certainly the fourteen people whose lives are briefly

sketched here do possess qualities of leadership. I have not
seen fit to pin any labels of my own upon them. I have
tried to look at each through the eyes of the honest reporter who happens also to be a long time "insider." What
I have seen is that there is indeed a unifying thread bind-
ing these men and women. And the honest reader will
just as surely find that thread without having to search
laboriously for it.

Elton C. Fax
New York, N.Y.

Contents

Contents

Illustrations follow page 57

Malcolm X

THE TALL LIGHT-BROWN MAN, his kinky red hair a bit longer than usual, wore an unfamiliar though neatly trimmed beard and mustache as he strode lightly into the room. He went straight to the podium and sat down. Behind the familiar glasses alert amber-brown eyes moved with experienced swiftness over those assembled. He was calm and completely self-possessed. By contrast, an electric tension filtered through the thick semicircle of reporters facing him. As representatives of the New York and the national press they were about to engage in a memorable interview with Malcolm X, just returned from Mecca.

It was 7 P.M., May 21, 1964, and Malcolm, true to custom, had arrived on time. Knowing his insistence upon punctuality, his followers and well-wishers had filled the Skyline Ballroom of Harlem's famed Hotel Theresa well in advance. All were anxious to hear what the outspoken Malcolm had to say about his recent experiences in the holy city of Islam. The murmur of voices died instantly as a reporter fired the opening question:

"Is it true, Minister Malcolm, that you *now* say you no longer believe all white people to be devils?"

The answer came swiftly and clearly:

"True, sir! My trip to Mecca has opened my eyes. I no longer subscribe to racism. I have adjusted my thinking to the point where I believe that whites are human beings . . ." Here Malcolm paused momentarily before adding, ". . . as long as this is borne out by their humane attitude toward Negroes."

Another reporter, resurrecting Malcolm's "racist" image, asked Malcolm if he were not still basically a racist.

"I'm *not* a racist. I'm not condemning whites for being whites, but for their *deeds*. I condemn what whites collectively have done to our people collectively."

Malcolm's smile was warm and captivating as he handled the harsh questions of a skeptical press with the skill of the honest thinker and world traveler he had become.

"Incredibel! Incredible!" murmured white reporter M. S. Handler of *The New York Times*. And incredible it was indeed for, as black writer Alex Haley later recalled, it was just a few years earlier out on the sidewalk, eight floors below, that Malcolm X had been a hustler and a peddler of dope.

It seemed that during the first half of Malcolm's life everything went wrong. Just about everything he did was wrong, and had he been an ordinary man the world would never have heard of him. But Malcolm X had three qualities that set him apart from the ordinary. He was highly intelligent; he was eager to learn; and, most important of all, he was a man who could and did change his behavior patterns from negative to positive, admitting as he moved ahead how wrong he had been.

The seventh of his father's thirteen children, Malcolm Little was born in Omaha, Nebraska, on May 19, 1925. His white-skinned mother, Louise, was from the West Indies. The daughter of a black woman and a white man, Louise had never known her father. In Philadelphia she had met and married Earl Little, a Baptist preacher from

Reynolds, Georgia. Actually, the Reverend Little was known as a "visiting preacher," one having no regular church of his own and who preached upon invitation from the pulpits of others.

Earl Little was a huge, powerfully built black man with barely four years of formal schooling. There had been violence in his life for he had lost an eye and three of his four brothers had been killed by white men. But Earl Little was not a frightened man. His fervent sermons were inspired by Marcus Garvey, a dynamic black orator who came from Jamaica to the United States in 1916 to organize chapters of his United Negro Improvement Association. *"Up you Mighty Race! You can Accomplish what you will!"* That was the Garvey rallying cry that attracted so many low income black Americans to the U.N.I.A. even as it frightened and angered so many whites. Earl Little quickly became a U.N.I.A. organizer, and though his Sunday sermons barely hinted his Garvey-inspired beliefs, his U.N.I.A. speeches during the week thundered straight down the Garvey line. The Littles moved from Omaha to Milwaukee and then to Lansing, Michigan, where the Reverend Little bought a modest home in a white neighborhood. That choice, along with his militant weekday activities as a Garvey organizer, did not sit well with the Black Legion, a local white terrorist group who kept Earl Little under close watch.

Malcolm was not five years old when he was suddenly wakened one night by a confusion of shouts and pistol shots. Smoke and flames began to pour from the house as the sharp cracking of Earl Little's pistol drove off two white men who had set his home afire. Luckily all the Littles escaped before the house collapsed in white-hot ruins.

With help from friends the family found temporary shelter and clothing until they could secure another house, this time in East Lansing. Malcolm had started to school. He was six years old when he was again wakened one night by his mother's screams. Police officers had come to tell her that her husband had met with a violent accident. A trolley car had passed over Earl Little's body. The huge man clung to life for more than two hours while local black citizens whispered that "Brother Little" had finally been put out of the way by hostile whites.

Proud Louise Little was alone with her eight children. Her widow's pension and welfare check were barely enough for them to exist upon so she found day work when and where she could get it. For about a year she was courted by a man who appeared to have the qualities of a good husband and father. This man bore a close resemblance to Earl Little, and Louise was considering herself lucky when he suddenly vanished. That was too much for Louise, who suffered a breakdown and had to be confined for the next twenty-five years to the State Mental Hospital at Kalamazoo. Her children became wards of the state, and while the two eldest were permitted to remain in their own house, the others were sent to foster homes. Malcolm had already been sent to live with a local black family named Gohannas. He was thirteen, tall, and defiant, and he began to misbehave in school.

When he went so far as to plant a thumbtack that his teacher sat upon he was promptly expelled. A state officer took Malcolm from the Gohannas home to a temporary detention home in Mason, twelve miles away. There he was to await transfer to reform school, an event that never materialized.

The Swerlins, a kindly white couple, in charge of the detention home, liked Malcolm. He did his chores well and, as he wrote years later in his autobiography, "it was out of their liking for me that I soon became accepted by them —as a mascot." But well meaning and pleasant as the Swerlins were, they and their friends thought nothing of holding conversations about "the niggers in Lansing" as though Malcolm could neither hear nor understand what they were talking about. Not once did they realize how deeply their remarks cut into the black boy's consciousness.

Through Mrs. Swerlin's influence Malcolm was enrolled in the Mason Junior High School where he was affectionately and popularly accepted as "the nigger" of his class. Fellow students and teachers who genuinely liked him never saw any harm in telling "nigger jokes" in his presence, while rival student cheering sections, watching Malcolm on the basketball court, "niggered" and "cooned" him throughout the game. Malcolm held his peace. He even became an outstanding student and, in the second semester of the seventh grade, was elected President of his class.

He was fourteen and an important event in his life was about to occur. Ella, his oldest half sister to whom he had been writing, came from Boston to visit. Ella was a large, proud, commanding jet-black woman. She looked, walked, and spoke with the firmness of their father, Earl Little, and Malcolm was impressed. Before leaving for Boston she declared that Malcolm simply must spend the coming summer with her. Ella had cleared it all in advance with the Swerlins. That was Ella.

It was Malcolm's first time so far from home. Never in his life had he seen as many black people as there were in Boston's Roxbury section. Ella, married for the second time, was complete mistress of her comfortable home. Active in church and club circles, she moved easily in Roxbury's upper-crust social set. By summer's end Malcolm was so enchanted by what he had seen in Boston he resolved that he would never spend his life in Mason, Michigan. An incident at school confirmed that resolve.

It happened in Mr. Ostrowski's English class. Malcolm

had done some of his best work in that teacher's class, so he did not hesitate, when asked what he wanted to do in life, to say he wanted to be a lawyer.

"A *lawyer?* Why that's no realistic goal for a *nigger,* Malcolm. You've got to think in terms of something you *can* be. Now you're good with your hands, so why not plan on being a carpenter."

Mr. Ostrowski was completely serious. Malcolm was crushed. He recalled that Mr. Ostrowski had encouraged the white boys and girls in whatever they said they wanted to do—even those whose grades were lower than his. From that moment on Malcolm began to withdraw from and distrust white people. He wasn't vocal in his feelings. He just sulked. Without a quarrel he left the Swerlins and lived for the remainder of the eighth grade with another family. And he wrote Ella that he wanted to return to Boston—to stay. In her typically swift and uncanny fashion Ella arranged to have legal custody of her brother and the very week he finished the eighth grade Malcolm Little again boarded the bus for Boston.

Ella was elated that Malcolm had wanted to come to live with her. She urged him not to look for work immediately but to move about on his own and get a feel of the city. Malcolm did just that. He rode and he walked through historic Boston, the theater district, and the university complex at Cambridge. But nothing held greater attraction for him than the poor black ghetto of Roxbury where people were so real and earthy. There the "chicks" were sleek and cute and the young "cats" wore sharp clothes, talked slangy jive talk, and "conked" their kinky hair straight. How different they were from Ella's sedate crowd up in Roxbury's Hill section.

One day Malcolm slipped into a pool room where the sharply draped hustlers idled about making bets on the games. A stocky black fellow called Shorty, who racked the balls on the tables, sauntered over. "Hi, Red." Shorty was warm and friendly. In a few moments the two were chatting like old neighbors, as indeed they were. Shorty was a high school dropout from Lansing, Michigan, ten years Malcolm's senior. He liked Malcolm at once, never suspecting that the tall redhead was so young. Shorty had ambitions. Though he was racking balls he also was taking saxophone lessons, hoping eventually to have his own band. When Malcolm confided his need for a job Shorty beamed.

"Okay, homeboy. If it's a 'slave' you want just leave it to ole Shorty and the boys. We'll look out for you. Ha ha ha ha! Boy, that oufit you're wearing is a solid mess. We *gotta* straighten you out—but quick!"

When Malcolm arrived home Ella had a message for him from Shorty. There was a job waiting for Malcolm in the men's room at Boston's famed Roseland State Ballroom. The shoeshine boy there had won some money and was quitting. Though Ella was unhappy about the job offer she let Malcolm take it hoping he would soon leave it for something else. But Malcolm was hypnotized and in a few weeks his whole life and personality had changed.

Gone were the country clothes and shoes he had worn to Boston, for Malcolm had gotten himself *sharp*. He began to wear "Zoot suits," with their long wide-lapeled coats and trousers ballooning at the knees and tight at the ankles. His bright expensive orange shoes turned up at the toes and the hat he wore had an extra wide brim. The kinky red hair was now a sleek, lay-em-down "conk" job, the result of burning it straight with a lethal paste made of lye and raw potatoes. And Malcolm was paying for all that on credit, out of earnings from shining shoes and selling reefers (marijuana cigarettes) on the side.

And that ballroom! It was Malcolm's heaven. While most of the dances were for whites there were also special functions for blacks. Malcolm, unable to resist the urge to be a customer upstairs when he should have been an employee downstairs, quit his job. But he wasn't worried. He had met and liked one girl in particular who had her own car and plenty of money to spend on him. Malcolm just *knew* he had it made. For several months until Pearl Harbor he flitted like a butterfly between odd "hustles" by day and by night darted like a moth in and out of dance halls and dives.

Meanwhile the army began to seize men so fast that Malcolm was offered just the kind of job he had been wanting. One of Ella's friends recommended him for a railroad job selling coffee and sandwiches between Boston and New York. Ella wanted to get Malcolm away from the girl and Malcolm wanted to keep the girl and see New York too, especially Harlem.

Malcolm was cheerfully aided by the train's cooks who always made a beeline to Harlem when in New York. They enjoyed having "Sandwich Red" along with them as they visited Smalls Paradise and other well-known night spots. And it wasn't long before Malcolm, playing much harder than he worked, was fired by the railroad company. He decided that he'd settle in New York for good as soon as he returned from a visit to his family in Michigan.

At the hospital Louise Little barely recognized her son. But it was his reappearance on the quiet streets of Mason that became a staggering experience for those who were quite unprepared for Malcolm's added height, conked head, wild clothes, and jive talk. Boys with whom he had been friendly in school were visibly impressed. But his old friends, the Swerlins, were so shocked they were glad to get him out of the house and on his way back east.

In New York, Malcolm easily found a job as a waiter in Smalls Paradise in Harlem. Handsome, affable, and polite, he became known to club patrons as "Detroit Red"; but he didn't last much longer than a year there either. Malcolm broke one of the cardinal rules of the club, that no employee was to hustle upon or impair the morals of a serviceman in uniform. So when he fell into a baited trap he was not only fired but barred from the club completely.

Faced now with the need to support himself in New York with the police breathing down his neck, Malcolm and a crony peddled marijuana cigarettes to musicians they knew were safe. To keep a jump ahead of the police Malcolm even secured a railroad pass enabling him to move quickly out of town when necessary. Then the draft board called him and Malcolm had a scheme all worked out. He showed up for induction in his wildest zoot suit and whispered to the examining psychiatrist that he was all set to organize a black fighting unit that would go down south and mop up all the "crackers." The army promptly rejected him.

Returning to hustle on the streets of New York and Boston, Malcolm began to carry a gun, for he was now dealing with tough hardened killers. He began also to sniff cocaine and was at low ebb when his old friend Shorty drove down from Boston to take him back and set him up in business. The "business" was a burglary ring made up of two white girls, Shorty, and Malcolm. They specialized in furs and jewelry which they stole from wealthy homes previously "cased" by the girls. It went smoothly until Malcolm tried to have a stolen watch repaired. When he returned to the jeweler's to claim it the detectives were waiting. They rounded up the gang and the girls drew relatively light sentences. Malcolm and Shorty drew ten years each, of which they both served seven. Malcolm was not yet twenty-one. Little did he or anyone know that he had already passed the halfway mark of his life.

Ella was Malcolm's first visitor at the Charlestown Prison, and throughout his confinement she never turned away from him. Inside the prison Malcolm, for the first time in his life, took serious notice of someone more scholarly than he. The man was a dignified, soft-spoken, black ex-burglar called Bimbi. Bimbi was the prison library's best customer and everyone, guards included, respected him. It was Bimbi who prompted Malcolm to read and to take a correspondence course in English.

Within two years Ella had effected Malcolm's transfer to the progressive Norfolk Massachusetts Prison Colony. There he continued to read and it was there he was visited by his brother Reginald and his sister Hilda. Reginald and Hilda were excited about the religion of The Nation of Islam headed by the Honorable Elijah Muhammad, a frail black man who called himself the Messenger of Allah. Elijah lived in Chicago and his followers, all black men, women, and children, were scattered throughout the black ghettos of the nation's large cities. Many, like Malcolm, were serving time in prisons. They called themselves Muslims and they neither smoked, drank, used narcotics, nor ate pork. Hilda and Reginald were Muslims.

Malcolm thought a long time about the Muslims before writing his first letter to Mr. Muhammad, who promptly replied, welcoming him into "the true knowledge." Thrilled beyond description Malcolm plunged fanatically into more reading. What he did not understand he soon learned by tediously copying every word and its definitions from the dictionary. This improved and stimulated his reading. Even after "lights out" he would sit on the floor of his cell reading and studying by the dim glow of the outside corridor light. He read world history, anthropology, and philosophy. He read the Holy Bible in its entirety. Malcolm read by that dim corridor light until he was forced to ask for a pair of prison-issued glasses. And he studiously corresponded regularly with Elijah Muhammad as he strictly obeyed the dietary and the abstinence laws of his new faith.

Elijah Muhammad's version of Islam differed vastly in many respects from that of Muslims elsewhere in the world, but Malcolm did not know that then. For instance, Mr. Muhammad taught that the white man was a devil who had raped and plundered the world's nonwhite peoples and their goods. Recalling his own grim childhood, Malcolm eagerly sought and found evidence in the books he read of the white man's exploitation of nonwhites. It was easy for him, with such evidence, to accept Mr. Muhammad's description of the white man as a devil. Malcolm's own experiences coupled with his newly acquired information of the world and his faith in Elijah's teachings made him a most formidable member of the prison's debating club. Moreover, he became a dedicated recruiter for The Nation of Islam among his fellow black prisoners. As far as Malcolm was concerned, the Honorable Elijah Muhammad could do no wrong.

Malcolm was released from prison in the summer of 1952 in the custody of his oldest brother, Wilfred, who had found a job for him in Detroit. Just before Labor Day he joined Reginald and Hilda in the tiny motorcade from Detroit to Chicago. They were on their way to hear Elijah Muhammad speak. Malcolm was transfixed by the diminutive, thin, light-brown man who praised him in his sermon and who afterward invited the entire Little family to dine with him at his home.

From that day on, Malcolm and Elijah became close associates, and within a year Mr. Muhammad asked Malcolm to address the brothers and sisters in Detroit in an informal and personal way. What happened must have been impressive, for Malcolm was immediately named Assistant Minister to Detroit Temple Number 1. Maintaining himself through honest work at the Ford Motor Plant, Malcolm continued to preach until his services as religious spokesman were requested full time. He was sent to Philadelphia, then to Boston where Ella, surprised but proud, went to hear him. Shorty, who was now doing well with his little band, was overjoyed to see Malcolm. But Malcolm's new-found faith drew a chilly reception from Shorty, who was not about to give up his string of women, whiskey, and pork chops for *anybody's* religion!

Through the sheer force of Malcolm's personality the temples he visited grew rapidly. Then Mr. Muhammad appointed him Minister of the important and struggling Temple Number 7 in New York City's Harlem. Back in the area of his old criminal haunts, a new Minister Malcolm X (he had dropped his surname, branding it a "slave name") looked up his old hustling cronies in the vain effort to convert them. He continued to "fish," however, and he was remarkably successful among the masses of hardworking, exploited black Harlemites who recognized his sincerity and the truth of much that he said. But there was more. Malcolm not only preached, he *lived* a doctrine of dedication to truth and justice and abstinence from all the evils he had embraced previously. He preached and he lived a doctrine of respect for women, particularly black women. And he preached and lived a doctrine of respect for civil authority when that authority respected his right to his religious beliefs.

Malcolm founded the now nationally distributed Muslim newspaper, *Muhammad Speaks*. While he was always immaculately clean and well groomed in conservatively cut clothes and was driven about in a smart car, his followers knew that Malcolm was not profiteering at their expense. Actually he owned nothing other than his clothes, a watch, and a typewriter. And he was still unmarried. His previous street experiences had taught him to be careful in relations with women. Then along came sister Betty X.

Sister Betty X was young, refined, college educated, and a devout Muslim. She was good looking, too. Malcolm liked her immediately, but he had Mr. Muhammad look her over and approve her before asking her to be his wife.

One night shortly after Malcolm and Betty were married two white policemen in Harlem, while breaking up a minor street scuffle, ordered bystanders to "get going." One man, Johnson Hinton, a Muslim, did not move fast enough, and the policemen split his skull with their clubs and hustled him off to the precinct. The news spread quickly to the headquarters of The Nation of Islam who dispatched Malcolm X and fifty of its husky, unarmed, neatly dressed Fruit of Islam guards to the scene.

The guards silently fell into an orderly ranks formation outside the precinct while an angry shouting crowd of citizens milled behind them. Malcolm entered the precinct and quietly demanded that the injured brother Hinton be hospitalized. Ignoring his demand, the police ordered Malcolm to "get that noisy mob away from the precinct." Malcolm countered that *his* Muslim brothers out there were silent, orderly, and disciplined. "That 'noisy mob,' " he told the police, "is *your* problem." After some hedging the police took Hinton to a nearby hospital where it was learned he had been seriously injured. However, when the word reached the crowd still milling outside the precinct that the hospitalized man was being properly taken care of the Muslim guard silently slipped away.

A jury later awarded Johnson Hinton a record $70,000 judgment against the City of New York, and Malcolm X and his Muslims became the talk of Harlem. Then Louis Lomax, a black journalist, asked Malcolm if the Muslims would permit a documentary film to be made for the Mike

Wallace Show. And C. Eric Lincoln, a black scholar, asked permission to interview and write what was to be his doctoral thesis on The Nation of Islam. Malcolm referred both requests to Mr. Muhammad, who cleared them with the understanding that the Muslims were to be presented in an honest manner.

The Mike Wallace Show was finally aired. Sensationally titled *The Hate That Hate Produced,* it was edited and presented in such a way as to shock white viewers into recalling mainly that Muslims were being taught to hate *them.* Dr. Lincoln's thesis, a serious piece of research, was quickly bought by a book publisher and given the shocker title, *The Black Muslims in America.* So the Muslims, whose leaders had unsparingly criticized white America's bigotry in the effort to lift themselves to a level of self-respect, became the talk of the nation. They also became known as *The Black Muslims,* a name they were never able to shake off.

Newspaper and magazine articles about them appeared in every major national and international publication. Malcolm X was invited to appear on national radio and T.V. networks and to speak at the nation's leading colleges and universities. Established black leaders and spokesmen were chosen and pitted against Malcolm in televised and nontelevised debates. Many of his black opponents were openly hostile to Malcolm and the Muslims. But Malcolm, always reluctant to please hostile whites by engaging in public verbal battles with his own people, never lost his composure in those forays. He was indeed such a cool and logical debater that even his most embittered foes had to grudgingly concede the validity of his arguments against American racism and bigotry.

He was becoming strong, but strong as he was Malcolm always acted and spoke as the agent of "The Honorable Elijah Muhammad," whom he adored. And though the frail leader fully recognized Malcolm's great talents (he had even sent him on a short trip to Africa) a rift began to grow between them. It broke into the open with the publication of a sensational United Press International story from Los Angeles, California, on July 3, 1963.

It was then reported that two former young secretaries of the sixty-seven-year-old Mr. Muhammad were lodging paternity suits against him. The disclosure rocked the Muslim ranks everywhere in America. It nearly devastated Malcolm. He investigated the charges on his own, even talking about them with Mr. Muhammad himself. No one with whom he spoke, including Elijah Muhammad, challenged or denied the U.P.I. story.

Brilliant student of human nature that he was, Malcolm knew that The Nation of Islam, in its state of shattered faith, would have to shift attention away from their exposed leader. They would, Malcolm reasoned, be forced to find a scapegoat. Four months and nineteen days later President John F. Kennedy was assassinated in Dallas, Texas. Mr. Muhammad issued swift orders that no Muslim minister was to make any public comment on that tragic event.

Malcolm, when asked by a reporter what he thought of the assassination, quickly rejoined that it was, as he saw it, "a case of chickens coming home to roost." The headlines screamed from coast to coast. White America read into the statement an unfeeling and sadistic expression of black hatred for not only the Kennedys but *for all other whites as well.* The Muslims, seizing upon their scapegoat, accused Malcolm of trying to undermine Mr. Muhammad for his own gain. Malcolm, publicly admitting that he had spoken unwisely, was swiftly silenced by Mr. Muhammad. He was not to speak either publicly or to his temple followers until further notice.

Former Muslim friends, including the heavyweight

champion Muhammad Ali, whose former name was Cassius Clay, began to avoid contact with Malcolm, and Malcolm openly declared that he knew that he was marked for death. But he was not finished. He quickly got down to the business of forming an organization of his own—one that would embrace black men of *all* religious faiths, and that would practice what the Muslims had mainly preached. In this effort he was not alone. Help came from a number of Muslims and, surprisingly, from many sympathetic whites. Then, with the aid of his sister Ella, Malcolm decided to make the pilgrimage to Mecca.

In Mecca he found true brotherhood among Muslims of all races and colors. White men were kind and helpful to him, one going so far as to give Malcolm the use of his home. Malcolm, profoundly moved, promptly wrote his famous "Letter From Mecca," admitting freely that he had been wrong in preaching that all white men were devils. Then he visited East and West Africa and Lebanon where, to his amazement, he found that he was well known. Everywhere he went he was enthusiastically greeted, except by the embassies of his own country.

Malcolm returned to America to spread the word of his new discoveries and experiences and what they had meant to him. He had not been home long before the house he and Betty and their four children occupied in New York (he owned no real estate) was fire-bombed. He received threatening phone calls. And the press, at large, far less flexible and honest than he, insisted upon linking his name with hate.

On Sunday afternoon, February 21, 1964, Malcolm X rose to address his followers at the Audubon Ballroom in New York City. A scuffle and angry voices drew attention momentarily away from the speaker's lectern, and in that instant several black men in the front row rose and shot Malcolm dead. They fled in the ensuing commotion.

For El-Hajj Malik El-Shabazz, the name Malcolm had
been given in Mecca, the end came as he had so often predicted.

Eulogies of the slain man poured in from everywhere—
not only from the entire Islamic world and from his immediate followers but from the hostile and conservative
black leaders who had been his severest critics. And as of
today, people the world over, especially *young* people who
believe in the dignity of all human beings, know and revere
Malcolm's name. Surely no greater tribute can be paid
any man.

Bayard Rustin

THE BODY OF Malcolm X was given a Muslim burial following services in one of Harlem's many Christian churches. Six hundred mourners had packed the Faith Temple Church of God in Christ on that bitter cold twenty-seventh day of February 1965. Among them, sitting alertly erect, was a tall, athletically built man with mahogany brown skin. His thick brush of gray hair, near-aquiline features, and elegant bearing made him distinctly noticeable in the throng. That man was Bayard Rustin.

No two men could have appeared less alike than Malcolm X and Bayard Rustin. Indeed no two men disagreed more than they did during most of Malcolm's brief career. Yet they shared much in common. Each, born and reared in northern urban poverty, knew what it was to be black in a climate of white racism. Malcolm, the rough-hewn street hustler, ex-convict, and convert to Islam, became an intelligent and highly articulate political and social dissenter. He dedicated himself to calling attention to what he saw as American injustice. College-trained Bayard Rustin, reared as a Quaker and a pacifist, had joined the Communist Party, and he also had served time in prison. Through brilliant civil rights stratagems and speeches he too had sought to correct his country's injustices. Each man had to contend not only with the white establishment but also with opposition from areas of black leadership. Like Malcolm, Rustin is one of America's most skillful and effective extemporaneous orators. He rarely, if ever, reads from a prepared script. And he has been known to open and close his magnificent addresses with appropriate songs which he sings in a moving and thoroughly professional tenor voice. Although what Malcolm X worked to attain and what Bayard Rustin still works to attain amount to the common wish to see oppressed peoples everywhere enjoy their human rights, there were marked differences in their personalities and hence in their methods.

Bayard Rustin was an out-of-wedlock child, born in 1910 in West Chester, Pennsylvania. He was reared by respectably poor grandparents. His grandmother, of Delaware Indian extraction, had been raised by Quakers and his grandfather, son of a Maryland slave, worked for the local Elks and did catering on the side. "Grandfather was well known for his turtle soup," Bayard often recalls with a laugh. Then he proceeds to describe an odd kind of family poverty quite familiar to black families whose breadwinners work for affluent whites: "We lived on a rich diet of party leftovers—turtle soup, roquefort cheese, lobsters, pies and cakes." He laughs.

But the table laden with rich leftovers did not keep Bayard from knowing he was poor and black. He had attended a completely segregated grammar school before entering an integrated high school in West Chester. In high school he not only made the football and track teams and played championship tennis, but was valedictorian of his class as well.

Following graduation from high school he drifted about the country studying for a time at the predominantly black Wilberforce University in Ohio, where he helped pay his expenses by singing in a quartet. Later, as a student at Cheyney State Teachers College, another black school in Pennsylvania, he continued to sing as a "single" while the group he left in Ohio went on to theatrical and recording fame as "The Charioteers."

It was 1938. America was still reeling from the blow delivered by the stock market crash eleven years before and Bayard Rustin, following similarly bright and disillusioned young people joined the Communist Party. The American Communist Party at that time had taken the initiative in seeking to bring an end to the nation's racist practices. The Party had also come out against the military aggressions of Hitler and Mussolini and young Rustin, the pacifist, felt he had found the right place in which to work.

Two years later he took up residence in New York to become an organizer for The Young Communist League. While in New York he enrolled in City College where he recruited evening school students for the League. To support himself and to give some small financial aid to the Party he became a successful singer in New York City's Cafe Society Downtown along with the late great folksingers Josh White and Leadbelly.

Bayard lived with an aunt in Harlem, and there he had a chance to see and to know that much publicized black community. He found it, alternately, beautiful and hideous, gay and terribly sad. Of Harlem he has said, "At one level, there *is* a strange sense of community—but on another level, there's an absolute isolation and loneliness. There's such a preying upon one another, a kind of necessary preying, but it's terrible." Bayard Rustin developed a hatred for the social system that creates Harlems and that hatred bound him to the Communist Party until 1941.

When the Hitler forces attacked Russia the Communist line took an abrupt turn. No longer was it a party advocating peace. "America," it shouted, "must open a second front in Europe to help the Russians." Rustin was shocked by the switch. His Indian grandmother's Quaker teachings would not permit him to accept the sudden switch of the Communist Party from peace to war. But even more was involved now for Rustin. He, who had been specially assigned by the Party to form a committee against discrimination in the armed forces, was ordered to give up his project. The new line called for *everybody* to get into the war on the side of Russia. Ending civilian and armed forces segregation no longer had a place in the program of the Communist Party! Rustin, unable to agree, left the Party.

This second disillusionment occasioned by his experience with the Communists added fuel to the fires of Rustin's discontent. Like many other sensitive young black people he found it extremely difficult to accept being simultaneously black and American. Malcolm X felt it too. Whereas Malcolm, by conking his hair straight and wearing wild zoot suits, had taken one form of refuge from the searing realities of being black, Bayard took quite another. As he himself has put it:

"I tell you, brother, I fought against it for years—against being American—in my speech, my manner, everything. It's a hard thing for a Negro to accept, being American, but you can't escape it."

The nation was at war and A. Philip Randolph, veteran organizer of the Brotherhood of Sleeping Car Porters, had organized his first March on Washington. His plan called for the marching of from fifty to a hundred thousand black Americans on the nation's capital—unless fair employment practices were established in America's defense industries. Rustin, in need of something constructive to do to fill the new void in his life, volunteered his services to Randolph. He became Youth Organizer for the March that never came off. President Franklin D. Roosevelt issued Executive Order 8802 banning discrimination in the war industries and establishing the Fair Employment Practices Committee. The order came less than two weeks before the unyielding Mr. Randolph had scheduled his march.

Meanwhile, pacifist Rustin, refusing induction into the Army chose prison rather than the work camp alternative offered the religious objector. For twenty-eight months he was an inmate in the Federal prison at Lewisburg, Pennsylvania. Recalling that harrowing experience he has said that the awful thing about prison is its boredom. To avoid boredom he taught himself to play the guitar. He also built himself a lute which he learned to play. And he did a lot of thinking.

At the end of World War II, Rustin planned and organized the first of the Freedom Rides. He called it the Journey of Reconciliation. In North Carolina he was arrested for sitting in the "white section" of a segregated bus, and served thirty brutal days on the chain gang for the offense. Later he wrote a series of newspaper articles on that experience which brought about the abolition of the chain gang in North Carolina. Rustin was to be jailed many times in similar cases and was once jailed in California on a morals charge. Still he pressed on in the struggle for civil rights.

Rustin held a special appeal to the young who readily identified with the older man whose seemingly loosely knit personal life and easy-going work habits coincided so well with their own. In 1955 when Martin Luther King, Jr., was leading his Montgomery, Alabama, bus boycott, Rustin went down to offer his services. His blue jeans and wild-looking hair were in marked contrast to the ministerial neatness of King and his friend Ralph Abernathy. It didn't take long, however, for the southern brothers and sisters to discover Rustin's worth. One of them was heard to remark, "That tall fella from up the road with all that hair and fancy talk may be funny-lookin' but, man *he sho can* work!"

The Rustin genius for organizing the fundamentals of the problem immediately asserted itself. Finding that there was no car pool for getting the bus-boycotting Montgomery workers to and from their jobs, he went to Birmingham and got the black steelworkers of that city to lend their automobiles to the cause.

It was Bayard Rustin who became Dr. King's research man and who drafted the plan for The Southern Christian Leadership Conference. And later when King was indicted on charges of fraud in connection with his income tax returns, Rustin directed his legal defense committee. That committee raised $150,000 with which it fought and won the case.

Talk with any young volunteers, black or white, who have worked with Bayard in New York and you will quickly learn how profoundly impressed they are by him. His uncanny ability to look casual and almost careless, and yet be so completely able to issue the *right* directives at the *right* moment was one thing they admired. Another was his knack for letting them feel he had faith in their abilities, and an understanding of their impatience. He was also wise enough to warn his young co-workers of the dangers inherent in their plans, then let them proceed, if he could not convince them of the weakness. He told them, "After all, you'll never learn until you've made mistakes." Then, wagging a slender forefinger and speaking in his familiar high tenor voice he would continue, "Whenever you are staging a demonstration protest you must bear in mind that the form and manner of your demonstration must be simple, direct, and *it must relate to what you are protesting.* Otherwise your protest demonstration will fail."

There was an occasion when Rustin's young and attractive secretary, Miss Tina Lawrence, organized a group, the East River CORE. The group hit upon the idea of tying up homebound traffic at the peak rush hour on New York's busy Triborough Bridge by dumping refuse on the roadway then sitting in the middle of it. "What are you protesting?" Rustin asked. When told it was a demonstration against segregated schools in New York City he advised against it. "It's too complicated," he said. "Besides your plan doesn't relate to segregated schools, and it could tie up an ambulance or a fire engine." Miss Lawrence asked if he wanted her to abandon the plan. "Not unless you're convinced of its lack of wisdom," Rustin replied. Miss Lawrence wasn't convinced.

The demonstration came off. Motorists trying to get home from work that spring afternoon were outraged and the newspaper headlines shrieked their disapproval at the inconsiderate, anarchistic militants of East River CORE.

They made no mention that the protesters were demonstrating against the city's segregated schools. Later, when the newspapers made much of the World's Fair "Stall-in," Tina Lawrence and her East River CORE group joined the national leadership in opposition to the scheme. They had learned a valuable lesson. And when they noted that their refusal to cooperate in the stall-in made no newspaper headlines they took further note of that additional lesson.

Oddly enough, however, Rustin, himself, could not resist the urge to protest personally the opening of the World's Fair while, as he put it, "one third of the country lived in poverty." So when he blocked the entrance to the New York Pavilion and was promptly arrested he saw his own error. The following morning he quickly described what he had done as no more than "pointless grasshopping."

Rustin's mentor, the venerable A. Philip Randolph was once moved to remark, "It's easy to get people's attention, what counts is getting their *interest*." And Rustin, recalling his earliest days with Randolph and a youthful mistake of his own, smiled wryly. It took place when President Truman officially ended discrimination in the armed forces. Rustin was a young man working under Mr. Randolph.

When the Truman order came through, Randolph immediately dismantled his Committee on Discrimination in the Armed Forces, much to the dismay of Rustin and the younger men who felt that Randolph was "out of step with the times." Mr. Randolph had Rustin call a 4 P.M. press conference for him which Rustin did. He also called one of his own for 10 A.M. that morning at which he severely criticized his mentor. For several years Randolph and Rustin did not see each other, but when they did Mr. Randolph rose from his chair, his hand extended. "Why Bayard!" he exclaimed, "Where on earth have you been?"

Bayard Rustin thoroughly understands the impatience of youth, though he is not always patient with young people who do not work under his supervision. He has, for instance, attacked what he calls the lack of politics among some of the young black activists.

"Anybody can say to white people, 'Roll over, we don't need you.' But that is not political expression. The alternative to politics is to cop out and talk about hair, about what name you want to be called, and about soul food. Wearing my hair Afrostyle, calling myself an Afro-American, and eating all the chitterlings I can find are not going to affect Congress."

When asked what he thought about college courses in soul music and poetry demanded by some black students he was equally caustic.

"Everyone knows that education for the Negro is inferior. Bring them into the university with the understanding that they must have remedial work they require. The easy way out is to let them have black courses and their own dormitories and give them degrees."

He went on to declare that soul courses are worthless in a harsh world where mathemtaics and the ability to read and write good English are a basic requirement.

Once after delivering a thoughtful, one-hour address on the theory of nonviolence to 122 members of the Harlem Peace Corps, Rustin was challenged by a young man in the audience. "Nonviolence," the young man contended "is outdated." "Would you not, therefore, consider constructive ways of violence, Mr. Rustin?" Obviously disappointed that he had not gotten through to his young audience, Rustin enumerated the three essentials necessary to successful guerrilla warfare.

"If you're going to have an underground, then you must have certain things. First, you must be near the border of a friendly country that is willing to supply you with arms. Second, you must have high mountains and jungles into which you can retreat. And third, you must have the majority of the people on your side."

Having set forth those requirements he concluded that it was obvious that the Negro in the United States does not have and will not in the foreseeable future have those advantages. Such is the brand of thinking that makes Bayard Rustin a valuable strategist in any mass movement of people.

Without a doubt, his most remarkable achievement in that area, the one through which his name has come to be publicly known and acclaimed, was his planning of the 1963 March on Washington. At that time and during his own efforts at speaking publicly in behalf of civil rights for black people, Malcolm X referred to the March as "that Farce on Washington." It was not, as Malcolm later acknowledged, a farce at all but one of the most carefully organized and executed mass demonstrations ever held in the country. Rustin conceived and masterminded the plan. But his open participation in the project of his own creation did not come about as a matter of natural consequence. Before he was allowed to function in the plan he designed Rustin had first to overcome a great deal of opposition from other black leaders. And that in view of the national background made the job more difficult and the achievement more noteworthy.

The twelve months preceding the March on Washington were significant to America and especially significant to her black communities. James Meredith was admitted to the University of Mississippi under Federal guard as white rebel terrorists rioted and managed to kill a nonrioting French news correspondent.

A handsome, young black heavyweight boxer from Kentucky with the unlikely name of Cassius Marcellus Clay and an unusual flair for showmanship sprang into the nation's news columns. Americans viewed him first with amusement, then with consternation, and finally with downright hatred as he loudly boasted through rhyme his beauty and his fighter's skills. What made him effective was that nobody beat him.

South Carolina's Clemson College enrolled its first black student, Harvey Gantt, and the University of Georgia graduated its first black students, Hamilton Holmes and Charlayne Hunter. Birmingham, Alabama, churned with white violence as nonviolent black marchers led by Martin Luther King, Jr., sought to desegregate that southern steel city. Local white citizens, aided by police commissioner "Bull" Connor's officers, their dogs, clubs, fire hoses, and electric cattle-prods mauled and tormented unarmed black demonstrators at will. The latter, many of them women and children, offered no physical resistance.

In Jackson, Mississippi, soft-spoken Medgar Evers, field secretary for the National Association for the Advancement of Colored People, was quietly and legally urging his people to use the vote. Late one night as he stepped from his car and started to enter his home an assassin, hidden in a nearby clump of bushes, gunned Medgar Evers down. And racial strife erupted in New York, Chicago, and in Maryland's Eastern Shore city of Cambridge.

The year 1963 marked the one hundredth anniversary of the Emancipation Proclamation, and it was sadly obvious that black Americans were nowhere near complete emancipation. The March on Washington, therefore, was designed to take place on that date to dramatize also the fact and the depth of the black American's frustration and discontent. In the words of Dr. King it was meant to say to the nation that "America has given the Negro people a bad check" and that check had to be redeemed if the nation expected to enjoy internal peace. And the demonstration was above all else, to be dignified and wholly non-violent.

It was not a new idea. As has been mentioned, A. Philip Randolph had threatened the Roosevelt administration with a similar demonstration twenty years earlier. But it was a *prodigious* idea. The very thought of bringing thousands and thousands of people, black and white, from all areas of the nation to Washington for a day to demonstrate without creating chaos, staggered the imagination.

They had to have transportation and they had to be fed. They would have to have cool water to drink because the March was scheduled for late August and Washington is notorious for its summer heat and humidity. There would have to be numerous portable comfort stations set up along the line of march. And there would also have to be first aid stations, ambulances, and emergency stations for lost children. In all of these items the cooperation and the assistance of the local police would be absolutely necessary.

Finally, as a safeguard against the possibility of violent

outbreaks the local police, augmented by segments of the armed forces had to be available. This became a particularly touchy issue as areas of the press, not especially friendly to black aspirations and particularly hostile to the idea of a mass demonstration of black people in the nation's capital, published dire warnings and suggestions of impending disaster.

The success or failure of the March would depend principally upon its planners. Who could do such a job? Aging A. Philip Randolph, leader of the Negro American Labor Council, turned to his younger protégé, Bayard Rustin. It was a natural and logical choice. Not only had Rustin proved his organizing skills, but this particular march had been his idea. An anguished outcry rose immediately from the ranks of other black leaders. Rustin, they clamored, was an ex-Communist, and that alone could kill the effectiveness of the project. Not only that, he had been a "draft dodger," they asserted and one with an unsavory reputation at that. None other than fun-loving Adam Clayton Powell previously threatened publicly to "expose" Rustin if Martin Luther King, Jr., had insisted upon using his services in one of his earlier demonstrations. So hostile to Rustin were the N.A.A.C.P.'s officers that they induced Roy Wilkins to go against him as Randolph sought to place him in command.

Then Rustin did what was typical of him. Ever sensitive to the vital issues, which in this case were the need for group harmony and the success of the March, he withdrew. The black leaders, much relieved, then named Randolph, himself, director of the March. Mr. Randolph graciously and promptly accepted with the understanding that he, alone, would have the power to name his own staff. The leaders agreed, and Randolph appointed Rustin to organize the March.

When Bayard Rustin went to work on the March he put

one of his prime techniques to the test. He proceeded to find ways of persuading the authorities to cooperate in a demonstration to which they were basically opposed. And his first talks were with the Washington police. Under the spell of his wisdom and personal charm the police found themselves going along with Rustin's well-laid plans before they could say no. Rustin knew well how to deal with police officials. It was he who had previously gotten cooperation from the New York City police, who lent him a sound truck for use in managing crowds as he led the first school boycott against the New York City Board of Education.

So what took place as a quarter million Americans of many faiths and of both races assembled in Washington on August 28, 1963, is recorded history. They gathered in a collective spirit of love and peace, and restraint to mount the greatest single citizens' demonstration this nation had ever seen. And they saw it take place without a single act of violence to mar it. They had come from Hollywood's and New York's glittering studios and stages. They had come from the nation's sports and political arenas. They had come also from the southern cotton fields, the midwestern prairies and the tree-lined New England towns.

They heard even if they could not see Martin Luther King, Jr., as he stood on the steps of the Lincoln Memorial and cried out, *"I have a dream today!"* And the man whose skillful planning made it possible moved efficiently and virtually unnoticed by the public as he kept the proceedings flowing smoothly. For Bayard Rustin the March on Washington was a great personal triumph. But Rustin, the free-lance organizing wizard was already looking toward the next assignment.

Some of his critics have spoken slightingly of his lack of a base organization from which to work. True, he has been a professional "loner" except for an association in his

youth with A. J. Mustie, A. Philip Randolph, and the late
Martin Luther King, Jr. And he does direct the A. Philip
Randolph Institute and the A. Philip Randolph Education Fund both of which he set up in 1965. Rustin works
with some of the nation's most diversified groups.
To the more traditional leaders, Rustin seems most
unorthodox. He publicly opposed Malcolm X and the
Muslims, declaring that while their grievances were valid
they offered no solutions of any political value. Yet, respecting Malcolm's intelligence and integrity, he honored
the slain leader in death. As the mentor and personal ad-
mirer of Stokely Carmichael, Rustin has been sharply
critical of the Carmichael political theory that the United
States is incapable of change, so why not just give up on
this hopeless country and raise cain. On the other hand,
Rustin has sternly admonished the nation's law enforcement agencies with these words:
"You cannot repress one tenth of the population, no
matter how badly elements of it behave, without threatening the civil liberties of everyone in the nation. Where
there are not civil liberties, we cannot have social progress.
That, I believe, is the problem before us."
During the record-setting strike of New York City's
teachers in 1967 Rustin outraged many parents in New
York's black communities by supporting the United Federation of Teachers and its President, Albert Shanker.
The Rustin belief is that what is bad for organized
workers is bad also for blacks who are mainly working people. And on this theme he has often said:
"Not a single bill affecting the poor, including the civil
rights legislation, could have got through Congress without the labor lobbyists in Washington. If Negroes all over
this country were making the $2.00 minimum wage de-
manded by the A.F.L.-C.I.O. we would have in our
pockets each year more money than has been spent to date

on the whole war on poverty. And all the war on poverty could not do for the *Lumpenproletariat* what trade unions have done by organizing the working poor."

During the March on Washington he was heard to remark, "Just think, if all the white unemployed in the coal mine areas were marching on Washington today!"

Such broad observations have prompted some to suggest that Bayard Rustin is not truly a "Negro leader." Indeed, the National Urban League's able director, Whitney Young, once said of Rustin, "Bayard Rustin is not a Negro leader because a Negro leader is head of a Negro organization. Rustin concurs with that definition. Moreover he thinks and writes and speaks in universal terms. Addressing a conference of the Anti-Defamation League of B'nai B'rith, Rustin had this to say on black-Jewish relations:

"But in these times of confusion I recommend to Jews what I recommend to myself in times of confusion. I go back and read the Jewish prophets, fundamentally Isaiah and Jeremiah. And I want you to know that if every Jew in the United States—not just a minority of extremists—called me a black nigger, and said, 'We don't need you to speak out against anti-Semitism in Poland, we can handle it ourselves,' I would not stop speaking out against anti-Semitism in Poland. I would continue to speak because I could do no other, because Isaiah and Jeremiah have taught me to be against injustice wherever it is, and first of all in myself . . . Remember that the issue can never be simply a problem of Jew and Gentile or black and white. The problem is man's inhumanity to man."

No words could more aptly describe the feelings and the philosophy of Bayard Rustin.

Whitney M. Young, Jr.

It can never be argued of Whitney Young as it has been of Bayard Rustin, that his work shifts him from one base to another. Since 1947 Young has been affiliated with the Urban League. The National Office of which he is Executive Director is the nerve center of one of the two most prestigious American organizations working for national progress through the nation's black communities. The other is the National Association for the Advancement of Colored People.

Whitney Young's designation as a "Negro leader," in the most meaningful sense of that abused label, is unchallenged among those who know leadership. He is relatively young and, like Bayard Rustin, he is highly intelligent, articulate, and balanced. He doesn't shout, indulge in name-calling, or pound tables with his ample fist. He doesn't have to, for he is quite sure of his ground.

Those who deal with him soon learn that he listens well, and when he speaks has something worthwhile to say. Whitney Young both listens and talks to some of the most powerful industrial and political forces in this country. His remarkable success with them has often roused the suspicions of some of the younger and more strident black

33

activists and their followers. But even they have been heard to admit privately that "Whitney was 'down with it' when it counted most."

Many popular journalists, reflecting the apprehensions many white Americans have of articulate blacks, embrace Young warmly. And they wrap him in the mantle of "moderation" they like to place upon black leaders they consider "safe." This annoys him. He asks, "How can I have moderate feelings about the inadequate employment, substandard housing, family instability, and poor health suffered by Negroes in this country, the richest nation on earth?" Those who have misapplied the term "moderate" have no answer. Those who know Whitney Young also know the answer.

His father, Whitney Young, Senior, a graduate of the Illinois School of Technology, had as a young man left a good job in the Ford Motor Plant to teach. Lincoln Institute at Lincoln Ridge was tightly segregated Kentucky's answer to the need of a boarding high school for the area's black children. It warmly welcomed the senior Young to its staff and in a short time Professor Young became Lincoln's President.

A son was born on the last day of July 1921 to Whitney and Laura Ray Young and they named him Whitney Moore Young, Jr. Little Whitney grew up in an atmosphere of family security. Though the family lived in the south, Whitney rarely heard his parents assail whites with bitterness and hate, either publicly or in their home. Both parents knew the value of learning and of living a life of love and charity, and they passed the tradition on to their son. Because the elder Youngs were teachers, they were able to overcome the poor school facilities for local black children by tutoring Whitney at home. That plus his own intelligence enabled him to get through high school by the time he was fourteen.

It was 1935 and the nation was caught fast in the grip of the great depression. Lincoln Institute was reeling under a debt of $10,000 and was about to close its doors. President Young, a man of optimism and faith, persuaded his black and white trustee board to hold off the closing for a few weeks. Then a miracle occurred. A black philanthropist in nearby Lexington died leaving $10,000 to the school. That gift was the fitting climax to President Young's "Plan Of Faith" that lifted him to the status of a seer in the eyes of his staff and students. Nor were his patience and valor in the face of disaster lost upon Whitney Jr. whose admiration of his father had begun early in his life.

"My father taught me and all of his students how to accept the unpleasant and to cope with it, instead of running away from it," he relates with obvious pride.

That Whitney Jr. did not grow up in the squalor of the slum or in the stifling atmosphere of the southern tenant farm did not mean he escaped the scourge of southern white racism. Indeed, he very soon learned how it eroded the spirit of the black male. His own father had often resorted to tricks used by every southern black man of the day to let white men see and hear what they wanted to see and hear from "their niggers." So whenever white trustees visited Lincoln Institute, President Young would hustle the boys out of the classrooms and out on the school's farm where they would pretend to be working the *soil* rather than working their *minds*. While the ruse, like that of fervently singing "those good old spirituals," always moved the white folks to weep and to open their wallets it was degrading to the black man's sense of honest and manly dealings. It was particularly distasteful to young Whitney who knew that such required behavior was designed to make black men believe that they were inferior to white men. It was a belief he had no intention of adopting.

Whitney was a tall, strikingly handsome youth. At Kentucky State College, a black school, he played basketball and was President of the senior class. He was only nineteen at graduation. Declining to join his father's staff at Lincoln Institute he wanted, instead, to study medicine. That of course required a lot of money for which he was quite willing to work. When he discovered that jobs in Louisville for which he had training and skills would not be open to him because of his color, he took such unskilled work as he could find. Working by day as a hotel bus boy and by night as a dishwasher he fell ill, quickly consumed his small savings, and had to abandon his dream of being a doctor. For a short time he took a job as a teacher-coach in Madisonville, Kentucky. Then, with the Japanese attack on Pearl Harbor in 1941, came another hope that he could study medicine.

The Army Specialist Training Program did give young men a chance to pursue medical careers. Whitney immediately applied for entry into the nation's two black medical schools, The Howard University Medical School in Washington, D.C., and Meharry Medical College in Nashville, Tennessee. Both were full and would be so until 1946. If he wanted to remain in the Army Specialist Training Program, Whitney would have to take a course in engineering at the Massachusetts Institute of Technology.

Three young black men were enrolled in the program at M.I.T., and the school authorities, having never before housed black students in its dormitory, were in a quandary. Should they put the trio together and be accused of setting up a jim crow dormitory section, or should they risk rousing the passions of bigoted whites by integrating them into the white group? They asked Whitney and the other two boys if they would be happier staying together. "No," they replied, "we would not."

Young's two roommates were white, one a native of Mississippi. At first there was silent hostility in the room between the black boy from Kentucky and the white boy from Mississippi. But within six months, Whitney recalls, "I was the best man at the southern boy's wedding."

The A.S.T.P. Program was soon abandoned after criticism that it was unfair to draftees already overseas. Whitney Young was assigned to the 369th Regiment Antiaircraft Artillery Group as a gunner. The company was completely black and was commanded by a white southern Captain. It could have gone badly for Young had the Captain, who was not as academically well prepared as he, disliked him. He liked Young, however, and in a short time the latter made First Sergeant.

But he was not beguiled by his personal success. He noted that while his white officers, recognizing his useful talents, were civil to *him*, they treated the lesser trained men of the company with arrogance and contempt. Whitney, having been brought up among black boys less fortunate than himself, knew how they felt and how to handle his superior training without alienating them. From their point of view he became "their man." Even more important, he knew how to evaluate properly the white officer's acceptance of him. At no time did Whitney Young ever forget who and what he was.

Meanwhile the regiment went to Europe and antagonism between the arrogant white officers and the black enlisted men took the form of clandestine attacks on the former by the latter. The officers, greatly outnumbered and on foreign soil, were terrified. Never before had they been obliged to deal with blacks who held the advantage. And Sergeant Young was called upon to mediate the differences. For the first time he saw black men in the position of power and he saw that in such situations white men were willing to negotiate with black men on equal terms. He later said, "It was this Army experience that decided me on getting into the race relations field after the war. Not just because I saw the problems but because I saw the potentials, too."

The year was 1947 and Whitney Young was out of the Army and enrolled at the University of Minnesota's School of Social Work where he earned his masters degree. He accepted the position of Director of Industrial Relations and Vocational Guidance at the St. Paul Urban League. During his three years there, recalling his inability to earlier obtain work suited to his skills, he opened St. Paul's streetcar lines, the taxicab company, and the sales counters of department stores to their first black employees.

From St. Paul he moved on to the Omaha, Nebraska, Urban League as its Executive Director. There he continued to hammer away at placing black workers in jobs they had not previously held. And he was invited to lecture at the School of Social Work at the University of Nebraska and to teach at Omaha's Creighton University.

On May 17, 1954, the U. S. Supreme Court declared, in a case involving *Brown vs. Board of Education of Topeka, Kansas,* that "Separate and equal facilities are inherently unequal." The ruling was a prelude to the later Supreme Court's order to all segregated schools in the United States to become desegregated "with all deliberate speed." Whitney Young was aroused by what was beginning to happen in Dixie. So with the urgings of the charming wife he had acquired and with more than "all deliberate speed" he accepted the Deanship of the School of Social Work at Atlanta University.

As the new Dean he began to work wonders. During his six years at Atlanta the School of Social Work doubled its enrollment. His students did their field work training in first-rate settlement house agencies and at first-rate hospitals for mental illness. Young's wizardry at fund-raising doubled the school's budget, and faculty salaries were upped 60 per cent. In recognition of such distinguished work Young was given the Florina Lasker Award at the 1959 National Conference of Social Workers. And he was only thirty-eight years old.

While Whitney Young's name was by no means familiar then to America at large it was well known to the field in which he worked so effectively. A large imposing man, he was an astonishing public speaker who never failed to captivate white audiences in particular with his warmth, incisive thinking, and good humor. He would melt frozen-faced listeners with the friendly way in which he'd describe how much more easy it is to integrate a house of pleasure than a house of worship. He directed his controlled anger not at white people as such but at the foolish and unthinking things they do to themselves and to the nation as they discriminate against nonwhites. He hadn't walked on picket lines, nor had he been pummeled and jailed for demonstrating. Still his was a voice heard and heeded by those affluent whites whose only previous contact with blacks was with the menials who served them. And he knew also how to address his own people.

Seeking to clarify his role to black audiences he would ask them, "which function is really more important for *me* to perform? Should I get on a Harlem street corner, cuss Whitey out, and tell the world what a real bad cat I am or should I go quietly down to General Motors and try to get jobs for ten thousand unemployed black men?"

On other occasions he'd say, "Man, you can't shoot, shout, or holler your way into power to save your life. *Somebody's* gotta get into those conference rooms downtown and talk sense to the man who *has* the power."

The Chairman of the Board of the National Urban League, Lindsley Kimball, heard Young and liked what he heard. He helped make a $15,000 Rockefeller grant for study at Harvard available to him. That was in 1960. The next year saw veteran Lester Granger retiring from the Executive Directorship of the League and Kimball approached Young about considering the vacancy. But Whitney had reservations.

At St. Paul and Omaha he had learned much about the organization's built-in conservatism. He knew that for fifty years the reputation of the Urban League was that of finding jobs for middle-class black Americans. Demands in the black communities now were for job opportunities for the lower classes. The National Office's budget was slightly over a quarter of a million dollars and the building carried a heavy mortgage. If he were to take the job he'd have to set a new policy. Yes, the challenges were enormous, but the Board of Directors wanted him, and Whitney Young became the Urban League's new National Director on August 1, 1961.

His army experience had taught him two vital lessons. One was that if you want to deal with a big organization you get to the top man as quickly as possible. The other was that when you had something the top man wanted you were in a position to bargain for what you wanted in return. Even before he tackled outside corporate industry, however, he did a job of renovating at home.

Making a point of visiting the League's local branches he opened four additional regional branches, bringing their total to five. In addition he established the League's Washington Bureau. The budget was $300,000 upon Young's arrival. Within his first year as national Director that figure was doubled. And the prospect for the early 1970s is a budget of $15 million. While not a membership organization like the N.A.A.C.P., the Urban

League does have a total of 115,000 combined board members, committee members, and volunteer members. And its three thousand paid employees keep its ninety-five local offices busy throughout the nation.

Young then moved in on big industry. Time, Inc., International Business Machines, Ford, American Telephone and Telegraph, and Kaiser Industries were ranking targets. He persuaded their head men that it was in the best interests of *their organizations* to join together with him in forming his Corporate Support Committee. Getting the nation's top industrial leaders interested in the black, urban, employable (but unemployed) Americans was a worthy move in a positive direction. He won friends for the League—friends with money power. Six years after he became the League's number one man *Time* in recognition of his achievements in the business community, invited him to join in a twelve-day tour of Eastern Europe with twenty-five business executives. Young thought at first that he was invited merely as a "showpiece" abroad. Before the tour ended, however, he was offered several corporation Vice-Presidencies. But what pleased him most of all was that from those twenty-five executives he was able to secure fifty thousand jobs for black workers. And just to ice the cake he received a check from Henry Ford II for $100,000 to spend as he wished. Young used that and similarly given monies to enlarge the League's national program. He was doing very well indeed with the men who controlled the nation's economic life.

At the same time, remembering again his army days, Whitney Young worked with the leaders and the foot soldiers of the civil rights movement. He had to make certain that his hobnobbing with wealthy corporation chiefs did not shut him from those whose immediate interests he was representing. First he had let his Urban League trustees know that they would have to support the 1963

March on Washington, the 1965 March from Selma to Montgomery, and the James Meredith March through Mississippi in 1966. And he did what he, personally, had never done before. He joined the demonstration in two of the marches.

Young learned early in his work that to convince the country's high-level businessmen of the truth of his claims of antiblack discrimination he must have facts to back his statements. So he did his homework *thoroughly* before going into conferences. When he stated that the income of the average black family is only 52 per cent of that of a white family he could prove it. He could also prove that while black people are 11 per cent of the total population they are allowed to live in only 4 per cent of the nation's residential areas. Black children receive three years less education than white children, and their parents die seven years earlier. Young uncovered these grim facts. And he was fully prepared to support the validity of his case when in 1963 he presented a proposal that, by bureaucratic government standards, was bold and unique.

The proposal was popularly known as the "Domestic Marshall Plan," and it was designed to give the black American a chance to catch up with the rest of the nation. "There's no way," Young said, "for the back wheels of the car to catch up with the front wheels if both are moving at the same rate." The plan called for the elimination of racial ghettos. It called for vastly improved health, education, employment, and welfare services. Young estimated that the cost would be high—quite possibly ten or twenty billion dollars a year. But he argues that a nation intelligent and rich enough to put men on the moon, could put its own disadvantaged citizens on their feet.

Many sections of the white community were shocked by the Young proposal. "Why should Negroes," they asked, "get special treatment? Why don't they pull themselves up by their bootstraps as we Jews, Italians, Irish, and other immigrant groups did?" Whitney Young calmly rejoined that black Americans were not voluntary immigrants to begin with. They were slaves. He further explained that there are advantages to having a white skin in a white-dominated society; that the changing of names and the "bobbing" of noses do not permit nonwhites to slip unnoticed into the dominant and accepted pattern of American whiteness.

He reminded white America of how the black family structure is weakened by society's suppression of the adult male head, who does not earn enough to support his dependents in dignity. And he cited that with limited earnings there were those restrictions on where blacks can live in most of our cities, preventing them from moving in significant numbers into the more desirable community developments.

Congress was not initially impressed with the plan. But it came at a time when attention was focused not only upon black demands but also upon the growth of the *power of black protest*. The nonviolent marches and demonstrations in Birmingham, Alabama, and the brutal way in which they were responded to by the police were winning sympathetic support among fair-minded Americans. Then there was the most impressively dignified March on Washington and its temporarily sobering effect upon the nation and its representatives in Washington. Both the Kennedy and Johnson administrations were persuaded to give limited measures of support to Young's plan. First, however, they changed its name. The program Young introduced to the country as *The Domestic Marshall Plan* became known as *The War on Poverty Program*.

But the misery that the plan was designed to erase did not begin to vanish quickly. Our country's citizens and its leaders, conditioned to looking for quick gimmick cures and solutions, were not willing to face up to the realities of a disease that had been progressing for three hundred years. While resistance to changes in the country's racial patterns remained high and black frustrations boiled to overflowing.

In August 1965 a riot erupted in the black ghetto of Los Angeles, California, called Watts. Within six days thirty-five people were killed, hundreds were injured, and property loss and damage soared into the millions. When asked by the press to comment on the disaster, Whitney Young replied that public officials obviously were completely unaware of conditions in that and similar black communities. A reporter asked Young if there had been a breakdown in communications between black and white he retorted that such was impossible. "How can there be a breakdown in something that has never existed?" He then recommended that the Urban League set up a three-year program to develop a black political leadership in the black community.

The program began in 1965 with a Rockefeller Foundation grant of nearly half-a-million dollars. During the following year Young called meetings in ten cities in the search for one thousand or more leaders who would form the kernel of neighborhood self-help units.

During the following summer of 1966 a $500 million World Trade Center was proposed for downtown New York City. Young felt that the huge expenditure could and should benefit New York's black community. Why not, he suggested, erect the proposed World Trade Center in Harlem? Blasé New Yorkers gasped in disbelief. Was the "moderate" Director of the National Urban League *serious?* He was. Young pointed out that the world's largest black community within a city was within easy commuting reach of all New York residents. Besides, the Center's location there would relieve the midtown traffic congestion; and it would bring commerce to the ghetto area, providing jobs for its black inhabitants.

The business community favored keeping the Trade Center downtown and a political squabble between Democrats and Republicans ensued over the proposal. By September, New York's Governor Rockefeller announced that while the downtown area would host the World Trade Center, Harlem, he had decided, would get a $20 million New York State office building. Whitney Young initially welcomed the plan. However, on closer study he concluded that a state office building would not mean as much to the residents of Harlem as its proponents had declared.

In the midst of his disappointment with Governor Rockefeller's proposal he took a trip to Vietnam to investigate the grave charges that 22 per cent of all American combat casualties there were black. Young was especially concerned inasmuch as it was rumored that many young black men had volunteered for combat duty out of boredom and frustration with conditions at home. Some, it was said, even volunteered to take on the most dangerous missions because of the pay that was in it.

In Vietnam, Young learned, after five days of talking with men in the battle zones, that the situation warranted official probing and correcting. Black soldiers were wounded and killed at a rate way out of proportion to their population ratio. They did indeed volunteer for Army service because they could do better financially there than as civilians at home. They did volunteer for hazardous assignments for the pay they couldn't earn at home. Black officers were scarce in the Army and even scarcer in the Navy and Marine Corps. Service facilities during off-duty hours were more or less segregated and the Army did nothing to correct the situation. Clashes between black and white servicemen were not rare. Whitney Young had the facts and figures proving his findings. Returning to

Washington he reported to President Johnson and he recommended strong and swift changes.

The year 1966 was one of unrest and violence in black communities. Riots and cries of Black Power frightened and angered many whites, who pressured their representatives in Washington to help bring an end to them. In the early fall Congressman Adam Clayton Powell was threatened with dismissal from his Chairmanship of the House Education and Labor Committee. Not only was he eventually relieved of his Chairmanship but also denied his seat in Congress. Whitney Young and other black leaders joined in protest until Congressman Powell was reseated.

The summer of 1967 brought the nation's business, labor, religious, and civil rights leaders together in Washington, D.C. The Urban Coalition, as it calls itself, had resolved to take such steps that were needed to cure the sickness of America's eruptive cities. Whitney Young was one of the meeting's participants. During the sessions New York City's Mayor John V. Lindsay and others suggested that the rioting of black slum dwellers might well bring about a backlash of white public opinion. Young made the following comment:

"The Negro has as much right to have his extremists as anybody else. Rap Brown did not cause unemployment in the country. Rap Brown did not put Negroes in ghettos. Rap Brown did not perpetuate upon Negroes inferior education. This was done by other people in the society and it is to the other people that we must look."

Still, opposition to Negro rights continued to make itself felt. A watered-down version of President Johnson's Civil Rights Bill was the best that could be obtained in Washington. And in New York City middle-class white voters, who rarely are the victims of police harassment, defeated an effort to retain a newly established Civilian

Complaint Review Board. The Board had been established as an independent civilian unit to investigate police infringement upon citizens' rights. The National Urban League, making its feelings known through Young, suggested that "when the Irish didn't like the way the police behaved, they didn't revolt. They joined the force and took it over." The inference was clear.

Undoubtedly Young's most amazing achievement as head of the Urban League has been to move it into the civil rights arena without changing its traditional mission. From its very beginning the League has sought equal opportunity for black Americans through *negotiation and persuasion*. That remains unchanged. Whitney Moore Young, Jr., imaginative, personable, and effective, has added something that is in keeping with the spirit of the approaching century. It is most clearly expressed in the following quote from one of his interviews: "The day of planning *for* the Negro is past. It is time the planning is done *with* him."

Coretta Scott King

ONE SCARCELY THINKS of Martin Luther King, Jr., without thinking also of his valiant widow, Coretta. Her handsome and noble likeness, appearing on the covers of major news periodicals during the past months, has become familiar to many peoples of the world. In previous years, however, only family and closest intimates knew what she contributed to the life and work of her martyred husband. So closely joined were their lives and their work as to create the appearance that, of the two of them, Martin was, in all considerations, the leading personality. Dr. King's greatness is unquestioned. A part of that greatness, it should be remembered, however, is reflected in the deliberate care with which he chose the woman who was to share his life with him. He was never more perceptive than when he made that choice.

Coretta King is a singularly remarkable woman, and a personality in her own right. This narrative, therefore, is not intended to be a recitation of her late husband's achievements with her name inserted for sentiment's sake. It is, instead, meant to relate briefly what a brave and able woman has added and is still adding to the promotion of love and decency in a troubled world.

Martin and Coretta King shared something in common with Whitney Young, Bayard Rustin, and toward the end of his life, Malcolm X. Each was dedicated to the pursuit of nonviolent resistance to racist-inspired injustice. That is why Whitney Young, who had never before joined a civil rights march, walked in the front ranks of that historic 1963 March on Washington. It was why Bayard Rustin suddenly appeared in Montgomery, Alabama, to offer his services to the Kings and to their followers. And it was why Malcolm X, who previously had mocked the March on Washington, later expressed admiration for the Kings and a disposition to work more closely with them.

It must be at all times remembered that Martin Luther King, Jr., was a *modern American revolutionary* who sought to change those things which he felt were harmful to America. His method, patterned after that of India's Mohandas K. Gandhi, was one of nonviolent direct action. His wife, Coretta, fully understood her husband, whose philosophy had become her own.

"Nonviolent direct action"—it was a phrase not readily understood by the public at large. They seized upon the adjectives "nonviolent direct" but they forgot or overlooked the vital noun "action." As to those who understood it best of all, the leaders themselves, it was the program of nonviolent direct action against American racist practices that brought and bound them so inextricably together. They often disagreed, as humans do, on *how* to reach the desired ends. But they were unanimous in their resolve to offer unceasing resistance to racial oppression, and it was in this resolve that the strength of Coretta King made itself felt.

Coretta Scott, her sister, Edythe, and brother, little Obie, were country children, having been born and reared on their paternal grandfather's farm. Old Granddaddy Jeff Scott was proud of his three-hundred-acre Alabama farm twelve miles outside the town of Marion. He and his wife, Cora, had toiled long hours in the field and they had cut and sold many a cord of pine wood in order to save enough for their land. The struggle struck Cora down and she died before she was forty-one. Old Jeff was killed in a car accident when he was sixty-eight.

Obadiah Scott, one of their thirteen children, was Coretta's father, and he built the house for his bride, Bernice McMurry Scott, in 1920. Everyone called him Obie and everyone respected the Scott family because they were hard-working and honest. One might describe them as living in a state of moderate and dignified poverty. They raised their own hogs, cows, chickens, cotton, and vegetables, and the children grew up learning how to do farm chores. Coretta helped feed the chickens and livestock and she milked the cows. Always a strong child, she hoed, "chopped," and picked cotton, well enough to earn extra money at it with which to help buy her school needs.

The nation was deep in the depression of the mid-1930s. Coretta, not yet in her teens, became aware of how black men of the south were kept in debt by unscrupulous white men. Her father's truck, for instance, was mortgaged to a man who took advantage of the situation by collecting more than was due him. But Obie Scott managed to get out of debt and even to establish credit at the local bank. Other black men of the area were not so fortunate, for Alabama during the 1930s was a mean and a tightly segregated state. Black men who stood up for their rights against white men often met violent death.

Church and school activities were most important in the lives of the Scotts and their neighbors. Indeed, the only social life for country people was to be found in the church. Because the Scotts and the McMurrys were active religionists it was natural that Coretta and her sister and brother would be brought up in Mount Tabor A.M.E.

Zion Church. Coretta recalls now that there was no "social gospel" preached from the pulpit of Mount Tabor. No one considered it befitting a preacher to discuss openly the plight of black sharecroppers in the rural south. That constituted standing up for one's rights, which could be fatal. The gospel preached, therefore, was one of obedience to God's will, and faith in the belief that the sower of evil seeds would automatically reap his evil harvest.

Now if one was a true and devout believer one did not grow impatient to see justice done. One knew that justice would come only in God's own good time. That was what black slaves had been taught by their masters to believe. Some never questioned it. Others felt it wise to protect themselves and their families while God was taking his own good time to punish the evildoers. Obie Scott was one of the latter. Like many of his neighbors he kept a loaded pistol in his home. Like his neighbors he had it nearby when in unfriendly territory. Yet everyone who knew Obie Scott knew he was a Christian gentleman.

Little Coretta's all-black school in the village of Heiberger was an unpainted, frame one room structure where more than one hundred children went from the first through sixth grades. The Scott children lived three miles from Heiberger and they walked back and forth to school each day, rain or shine. White children, meanwhile, rode to their school in buses. Inside Coretta's school a wood-burning stove provided heat. The rough desks and benches had been built by a local carpenter. A section of the wall painted black served as a blackboard, and the toilets were outdoors. The two black women who taught in that school extended themselves in the effort to make up for what the school lacked in equipment and comfort. Coretta Scott and her schoolmates learned early that in education, as in everything else black people experience, "separate" certainly did not mean "equal."

When they had completed the sixth grade, Edythe Scott, her younger sister, Coretta, and, later, Obie Jr. were sent to Marion to attend the Lincoln High School. As nearly every other school for black children, it had been named for "Honest Abe," and Lincoln High was semiprivate, originally established for former slave children. Its staff was half white, half black, the former mostly northern missionaries. And while the tuition was only four and a half dollars a year the Scotts had to sacrifice to provide that opportunity for their children inasmuch as they also had to be boarded with a black family in Marion. White children of their area, meanwhile, were bused daily in and out of Marion at county expense. Nor did they miss a chance to taunt and harass the black students whenever the two chanced to meet. Coretta was not loath to fight back.

It was at Lincoln that Coretta seriously began to study music, of which she was quite certain she would make a career. All of the students in Olive Williams' music class at Lincoln had to learn to read music. Miss Williams, a graduate of Howard University, who played piano and sang, brooked no nonsense in her class. Coretta adored her teacher. With a little voice coaching she extended the singing she had always done to the point where she performed vocal solos. She learned to play the beginning repertoire of all new pianists and at fifteen she was choir director and pianist for her church. From another teacher at Lincoln she learned to blow the trumpet.

Both Scott girls were musical, and Edythe sang with the Lincoln School Little Chorus. The Chorus made a tour of midwestern colleges, including Antioch College at Yellow Springs, Ohio. When, two years later, Edythe was graduated Valedictorian of her class at Lincoln, Antioch, remembering the Chorus, offered a full year scholarship to a worthy Lincoln graduate. Edythe Scott won it.

Edythe's letters home glowed with enthusiasm for her northern experience—her first away from the south. She purposely did not mention, especially in her letters to Coretta, the subtler kind of prejudice often indulged in by northern whites who think they have no racial bias. Very studiously did she avoid telling Coretta how self-conscious many of the white Antioch students were in her presence—how they fidgeted and talked only of the race problem. Nor did she mention that in spite of her good looks only twice was she asked on a date by a white fellow.

So Coretta, with only the glowing reports as her guide, could scarcely wait to join her older sister at the famed Ohio college. Antioch at that time had but six black students enrolled. Coretta's first year there was made easier than it would otherwise have been because Edythe was there with her. But then Edythe left to take her senior year studies at Ohio State University, and Coretta was on her own. Then it was that she discovered for herself all the attitudes that Edythe had not previously divulged. She found faculty members and schoolmates who, while believing firmly that black people were inferior to whites, would quickly add, "But Corrie, *you're different.*" At the same time they took it for granted that Coretta would date the lone black male student. She never did. Why, she asked herself, should she date him simply to affirm the assumption of her biased white schoolmates.

There were other problems. As Antioch's first black major in elementary education she encountered difficulty when it was her time to become a practice teacher of music in the local elementary public school. Whereas she had done a year of successful practice teaching at the Antioch private school, the public school board balked at having her. Her supervisor of practice teaching at Antioch gave her no backing nor did the President of Antioch. So the only courses open were for Coretta to teach in the wholly segregated school in Xenia, Ohio, or to teach for another year at the Antioch private school. She chose the latter.

Although these brushes with discrimination irked her, Coretta began, for the first time, to see that she was a person of worth. Contrary to what racism had been telling her and other black people about their deficiencies, she now *knew* she was not deficient simply because she was not white. Her white schoolmates had the same deficiencies themselves. Moreover, she reasoned that nobody ever goes to such great lengths to oppress or to retard a basically inferior person. His own inferiority will retard him without any outside help. And this was a vital realization indeed for her to take with her from Antioch in 1951.

Coretta's continued interest in music had been kept alive by two Antioch faculty members who advised her to apply for a scholarship to the New England Conservatory of Music in Boston. There she would major in voice training and, though she didn't know it, still another major change in Coretta Scott's life was already taking root. In Boston she lived and worked in the home of a wealthy patron of Antioch College. She did housework where she lived to help defray her expenses until she found another job through the local Urban League. This job was with a mail order house. Meanwhile a friend at the conservatory, Mary Powell, introduced her to a young Baptist minister working on his doctorate at Boston University. He, like Mary, was from Atlanta, and his name was Martin Luther King, Jr.

Actually Mary Powell had been doing a little quiet advance matchmaking, for Martin had asked her if she knew any nice girls he could meet. Mary mentioned two, of whom Coretta was one. She gave Coretta a splendid recommendation, mentioning her intelligence, talent, and good looks. But she did warn her friend Martin that Coretta Scott was not overly religious, and perhaps not what he had in mind. Martin didn't mind that it seemed, as he asked for Coretta's phone number. When he called her she remembered the glowing things Mary Powell had told her about him, and Coretta had no hesitancy whatever in agreeing to a luncheon date for the following day.

How different these two young people were! Coretta was a healthy, strong, attractive girl from the rural south, in Boston to begin a career as a professional singer. She and her family had made numerous personal sacrifices so that she could bridge the gap between their Alabama farm homestead and visions of the concert stage. Martin, serious and completely poised, was a young urbanite from Atlanta. Coming from a respected and relatively comfortable family, he knew exactly where he was going. He knew also what he wanted.

On that first date with Coretta he declared, "You have everything I want in a wife, character, intelligence, personality, and beauty." Coretta was at once charmed and bewildered. She was planning a career in music and had no thought of becoming a clergyman's wife. But Martin Luther King, Jr., was no ordinary man even if he was a clergyman, and Coretta continued to see him. She heard him preach in Roxbury and she was impressed. The things he said had great meaning to her and she began wanting to impress him and to please him, even in such matters as her selection of styles and colors in dress.

Then Martin invited her to Atlanta to meet his family and to visit the Ebenezer Baptist Church of which his father, the Reverend Martin L. King, Sr., is pastor. It did not take Coretta long to discover that Martin's father, a remarkably strong man, was quite particular about his son's associations with women. In fact, he told Coretta that Martin had a lot to offer the world and that any young woman in whom he might become interested should be fully aware of his abilities. Coretta, proud and spirited, was piqued by the suggestion that Daddy King felt that she was perhaps not good enough for Martin. In a manner and tone quite firm and polite she let him know, right then and there, that she also had something of value to offer the world. Somewhat surprised by Coretta's self-assured and fearless defense of her abilities, Daddy King took a second look at the young woman.

This was no ordinary pretty country girl seeking to set a snare for an eligible and secure young man from the big city. He was impressed and he never forgot that initial meeting and confrontation with Coretta Scott. Later, when Martin announced his intention to marry Coretta, his father was with him all the way; for it was none other than Daddy King, himself, who performed the ceremony at the home of the bride's parents on June 18, 1953.

During the first year of their marriage Coretta and Martin completed their studies in Boston. They lived in a four-room apartment, where Martin prepared his thesis in the den room. Coretta studied in the bedroom and made a point, in consideration of Martin's need to study, of never practicing her singing at home. She always confined that part of her work to the studios at the conservatory. Coretta was handling a schedule of thirteen courses, including voice, choir directing, and work with several instruments aside from the piano. Whenever she was late getting home, and that happened frequently, her husband would have a typical soul food dinner waiting complete with greens and sundry parts of the hog that many Americans don't realize are not simply edible but delicious. Nor was it at all unusual for Martin to assist with the housework.

Came the winter of 1954, and Martin's academic work was about complete. He had received several offers of work, including college teaching posts, but the Christian ministry was his first love. So he accepted invitations to

preach trial sermons in Detroit, Chattanooga, and in Montgomery. Each church in which he spoke wanted him to become its regular pastor, and it was not easy for him to
make a final decision. Coretta had hoped he would want
to remain in the north for a while where he would have
more freedom to develop his ideas. But Martin felt he was
more needed in the south, and he was particularly attracted to Montgomery's Dexter Avenue Baptist Church.
After preaching there several times during the year he
was ready to move in officially on the first Sunday in Sept-
tember 1954.

Coretta was quite prepared that Sunday when Martin
called upon her to address the congregation briefly. Dexter was a smaller church than Ebenezer, where Martin
grew up. It seated only four hundred as compared to
Ebenezer's seven hundred. But its well-educated and relatively affluent members appreciated the cultivation and
the poise of their new minister's wife. "My, how *young*
she is," many remarked. Coretta was young but so also was
Martin. Neither was yet twenty-six, but Martin at twenty-
five radiated a mature inner wisdom that made him appear older and therefore quite acceptable as a leader to
this discriminating congregation at Montgomery.

Coretta was Martin's secretary. She was also a member
of his choir, served on several church committees, re-
hearsed for her own concerts out of town, and performed
the duties of a housewife. As the hostess of the parsonage
she made friends, of whom Ralph and Juanita Abernathy
became their closest. Ralph, pastor of Montgomery's First
Baptist Church, was later to become Martin's most trusted
aide. Before 1954 was over two births were destined to
touch profoundly the lives of Coretta and Martin King.
The first was that of their daughter, Yolanda Denise, on
November 17, 1954. Less than three weeks later a mild-
mannered black woman with aching feet unwittingly pre-

cipitated the birth of the Montgomery Freedom Movement.

Rosa Parks was a forty-two-year-old seamstress. On December 1, 1954, she boarded a bus in Montgomery and dutifully took a seat at the head of the "Negro section." At the next stop a number of white passengers boarded—quickly filling the "white section." The driver, noting a white man standing near Mrs. Parks, ordered her to surrender her seat to the man—a practice that at one time was common in the south. But it wasn't Mrs. Parks' day to behave in the traditional manner, and she refused to budge. The driver called a policeman, who placed Mrs. Parks under arrest. From the police station Mrs. Parks called E. D. Nixon to come and bail her out.

Mr. Nixon, a strong civil rights worker and unionist active in A. Philip Randolph's Brotherhood of Sleeping Car Porters, was furious. He called Martin and Ralph Abernathy and the three of them decided to organize a boycott against the northern-owned Montgomery City Bus Lines Corporation. Coretta, confined to the house with her infant baby, was limited in what she could do but she did make and answer the hundreds of phone calls that coordinated the plan. That the boycott was just about 100 per cent successful was due as much to her work as coordinator as to the organization of it by the three men.

Montgomery city officials were so enraged they had Martin picked up and jailed for driving thirty miles an hour in a twenty-five-mile zone. His home was bombed also, but luckily no one was hurt. What happened was that Martin became at twenty-seven a national figure, visited and aided by such able men as Ralph Bunche, Roy Wilkins, Kenneth Clark, and Bayard Rustin. Talks and meetings that were to shape the pattern of the civil rights movement of the next few years took place in the King home under Coretta's understanding and expert supervision.

And on December 26, 1956, the U. S. Supreme Court ordered Montgomery to desegregate its buses.

Time magazine ran its first cover story about Martin on February 18, 1957, and the following month he and Coretta flew to Ghana with other black American leaders. Dr. Nkrumah had invited them to the celebration of his country's independence. Two years later they were invited to India by the Gandhi Peace Foundation. But while Martin and Coretta were sought after and honored by foreign dignitaries, who genuinely admired what they were doing, it was a different story altogether back home. Martin was jailed in Montgomery on the flimsiest charges while Coretta always bore the brunt of telephone harassment by cranks and hatemongers.

They left Montgomery in 1960, after six productive years at the Dexter Avenue Baptist Church, to resume their work in civil rights in Atlanta, Georgia. No sooner had they settled in Atlanta than a vindictive Montgomery grand jury indicted Martin on a charge of falsifying his income-tax return. The indictment implied that Martin had received and misused monies from two civil rights organizations. Again the tranquility of family life was disrupted with anxious meetings and conferences, with Coretta in the role of aide, advisor, hostess, wife, and mother. Though it was a hard life, powerful friends had rallied to Martin's defense, and he was fully acquitted.

The year 1961! This was the year of sit-ins by black southern students. They sat quietly at segregated "white" lunch counters and in "white" restaurants until either forcibly removed to jails or served. Rarely indeed were they served. Martin led sit-ins in Atlanta and was arrested so often his wife and family had come to understand that they could never be sure he would return home at the end of a day.

He and Coretta had two children now. Yolanda—or

Yoki, as they called her—was five and Marty, three. As the children heard and saw the news of their father's frequent arrests on radio and television they were curious. Why, they asked, did *their* daddy have to go to jail? Coretta explained to them that their daddy was a brave and a kind man who went to jail to help people. Some people, she told them, had no decent homes to live in, not enough food to eat, and not enough clothing to wear. "Daddy went to jail so all people could have the things they badly need. Don't worry. He'll be coming back." After that whenever another child would taunt Yoki about her father's jailing she would proudly reply, "Yes, my daddy goes to jail to help people."

At a later time, when Marty was in the third grade of an integrated school, a white classmate asked, "Is your father that famous nigger?" "The word is Negro," Marty replied with no further comment. Their mother had coached her children well. Moreover, Coretta King had succeeded in teaching her children a lesson about beauty that most Americans never seem to learn. She convinced them that there is more than one standard of beauty among humans in this vast world and that the Hollywood standard is never applied to all the earth's peoples by anyone who really knows what human beauty is.

Yoki was eight years old when Coretta was invited to Geneva, Switzerland, as an American delegate to the Women's International League for Peace and Freedom. The group, representing all areas of the world, including the Soviet Union, was pushing for a nuclear test-ban treaty. Coretta recalls rather sadly that when the women met with our government's representative in Geneva, they were brusquely told by him that they should have gone to speak to the Russian delegation, not to him. The Russians, he told them, were the ones standing in the way of a test ban. Coretta and the delegation went to the Russians, and, while they had no illusions of extracting the promise of a ban, they did get something their own representative did not offer. The Russians offered them the courtesy of a pleasant and polite discussion.

Back home, Martin was busy as co-pastor of Atlanta's Ebenezer Baptist Church. The sit-ins, backed by the Southern Christian Leadership Conference (S.C.L.C.), had reached Birmingham, Alabama. Martin had led a protest march into downtown Birmingham, and, along with Ralph Abernathy and others, had been jailed and held incommunicado for several days. This time Coretta was worried. A native of Alabama, she knew and understood the temper of its white people. And Birmingham had a particularly bad reputation.

Had Martin and the others been killed? In sheer desperation she put in a telephone call to President Kennedy in Washington. Unable to reach the President she did talk with his brother, Attorney General Robert Kennedy, who promised to do what he could. Twenty-four long and anxious hours dragged by with still no word of the imprisoned men. Then Coretta had a call from the White House. It was President Kennedy apologizing for not getting to her sooner and assuring her Martin and the others were all right. She would hear something further shortly, the President assured her.

Fifteen minutes later Martin called Coretta from the Birmingham jail and shortly thereafter he and Abernathy were released. When Martin arrived home and his wife told him about her call from the President, he smiled. "So *that's* why they hustled us out of jail so quickly. We wondered what had happened." Their jailing was by no means without its rewards. Birmingham city officials and merchants lost little time in sitting down with black leadership and negotiating a settlement.

For Coretta King the balance of 1963 was in turn depressing, exalting, and all but devastating. On June 12 Medgar Evers, N.A.A.C.P. leader, was shot dead from ambush as he started to enter his home. Coretta knew Medgar, his wife and their children, and for weeks she deeply felt the cruel blow of the family loss. Then her spirit soared to great heights on August 28 as she stood near Martin on the steps of the Lincoln Memorial in Washington. His voice was resolute and strong: "I say to you today, my friends, that even though we face the difficulties of today and tomorrow, I still have a dream."

Then again, tragedy. Three weeks later four little Sunday School girls died suddenly and violently when their Birmingham church was bombed by unknown persons. And finally, on November 22, voices of the nation's and the world's newscasters sorrowfully proclaimed the death by violence of President John Fitzgerald Kennedy on a street in Dallas, Texas. It would be a long time before Coretta King could no longer recall the President's voice, reassuring her Martin was all right in that Birmingham jail.

One year later Coretta accompanied Martin to Oslo, Norway, where he received the renowned Nobel Peace Prize. When they returned home Coretta gave the first of her Freedom Concerts. The concert, an eight-part performance of alternate narrating and singing was the story of the Freedom Struggle from 1955 to 1965. This first one was held at New York City's Town Hall on November 14, 1964, and it netted six thousand dollars. Beneficiaries were the Southern Christian Leadership Conference and the Goodman-Chaney-Schwerner Fund. Andrew Goodman, James Chaney, and Michael Schwerner were three young civil rights activists who were murdered five months previously by racists of Philadelphia, Mississippi. Coretta gave subsequent Freedom Concerts which, much to her

husband's surprise, contributed more than $50,000 to
S.C.L.C. and its various affiliates.

Another year and another temporary move was in the
making for the King family. This time it was to Chicago,
where Coretta set up an apartment in the south side slums
for Martin and their children, who by now had increased
to four. The fresh paint and curtains did little to make the
apartment attractive. Still, Martin and his family, there
by choice, believed their presence as residents could be of
help in improving ghetto living. They conducted work-
shops, led demonstrations (even at the Chicago City Hall),
and were caught in the middle of a riot. By this time each
of the King children, thoroughly briefed by their mother
on what their father was seeking to do for humanity, took
their disruptive life in stride. They had even been told
that death hovered close by their father at all times, that
death met in pursuits such as his was redemptive.

In the months preceding Martin's death Coretta detected a sense of urgency in him she had not seen before.
He was preparing his staff to "carry on in the event anything should happen to me." His Poor Peoples Campaign
was interrupted by trouble in Memphis, Tennessee. Black
sanitation workers there were striking for better wages
and working conditions and were bitterly opposed by the
city's Mayor and other municipal officials. In their desperation they called upon Martin for help. Yes, he would
come and lend his support but he would take a few days'
rest first. Demands on his time were such that he had to
slip off, leaving his whereabouts known only to Coretta.
On this occasion, however, he did something that for him
was unusual. He sent Coretta a bouquet of artificial red
carnations. Never before had he sent her anything but
natural flowers. This time, however, he explained that he
wanted her to have flowers from him that she could al-

ways keep and admire. Twenty-four days later Martin was shot to death in Memphis.

Yoki asked her mother if she should hate the man who killed her father. "No, darling, your daddy wouldn't want you to do that." Yoki quickly dried her tears. Harry Belafonte, a close family friend, suggested to Coretta King that Martin's scheduled March in Memphis should proceed and that she should lead it. On the day before Martin's funeral, Coretta and her three oldest children led that parade in Memphis. And she spoke with a controlled eloquence to the thousands who had come to keep faith with the principles of a martyred leader.

In Washington, Coretta King led the Solidarity Day March. Looking out from the steps of the Lincoln Memorial over the wooden shacks that formed Resurrection City she gave words of hope to the poor, who had been given little else as they camped in the capital of the world's richest nation. During the months since Martin's death Coretta King has written a book, *My Life With Martin Luther King*. Along with rearing her children she has found the time and energy to join other famous Americans in expressing opposition to our military action in Vietnam. In this she has remained constant to her and Martin's commitment to nonviolent resistance.

"The problems of racism, poverty, and war can all be summarized with one word, 'violence,' which seems to be fashionable in our society." The voice is musical and firm as she continues, "If we do not stop this madness, we will certainly destroy ourselves and the whole world."

A bereaved widow? Coretta Scott King is no mere widow of a famous martyr. She is a world citizen of great strength and compassion from whom we can all draw some measure of inspiration.

Roy Wilkins

THE AUGUST WAS WARM, and the multitude was soberly festive. A quarter million strong, they stood, knelt, sat, and reclined on the humid earth. Many dipped their hot and tired feet in the cooling water of the lagoon facing the Lincoln Memorial. As Master of Ceremonies A. Philip Randolph introduced the next speaker the crowd roared its approving response. And a slender, slightly stoop-shouldered brown man approached the bouquet of microphones.

"Thank you, Mr. Randolph . . . First of all, I want to thank all of you for coming here today because you saved me from being a liar. I *told* them you would be here. They didn't believe me because you always make up your mind at the *last minute!* (A great shout of laughter) And you had me scared! . . . But isn't it a great day? (A roar of assent) I want some of you to help me win a bet. I want everybody out here in the open to keep quiet and I want to hear a yell and a thunder from all those people who are out under the trees. Let's hear you! (Another tumultuous roar) . . . Yes, there's one of them *in* the tree! (More laughter)"

The speaker grew sober as he cited that procedures,

protocol, and rules exist to *enable* Congress to legislate, not to *prevent* legislation. He stated that the marchers wanted a Civil Rights Bill. And he thanked those lawmakers who had pushed for civil rights. Then, addressing those southern legislators "who want to pass a Civil Rights Bill but who don't *dare* to," he said this: "Just give us a little time and one of these days we'll emancipate *you!*" (Thunderous laughter and applause.)

For Roy Wilkins, head of the National Association for Advancement of Colored People, it was indeed a great day. It was a day that revealed something to the world about America that he had for many years believed. He was certain that racism could weld a massive force of black and white Americans together in a strong and dignified demonstration of protest. And it had. Yes, that record-setting March on Washington of 1963 had invoked the folksy humor in Mr. Wilkins that seldom shows itself publicly. Moreover, it had whetted the edge of his wit. And wit, as opposed to humor, is sharp—and often cutting.

Life for Roy Wilkins began in St. Louis, Missouri, on August 30, 1901. His father, born and reared on a share-cropper's farm in Mississippi, had attended Rust College. But William Wilkins' formal education was no asset to him as far as Holly Springs, Mississippi, whites were concerned. If anything it hurt him, for in their view he was an "uppity" black boy whose influences would spoil their "good niggers." So the elder Wilkins was forced to form a close alliance with a mule and a plow before fleeing to St. Louis, where Roy was born.

Roy's mother died when he was four. He, his younger brother, and their sister were taken to St. Paul, Minnesota, to live with an uncle and an aunt. Uncle Samuel Williams worked as the special carman of the private railroad car belonging to the President of the Northern Pacific Railroad. He was told that he had a big and important position, though Samuel Williams was paid only eighty-five dollars a month. It was scarcely enough to give him delusions of grandeur. Sam Williams exerted a strong influence on young Roy, who learned from him the value of hard work and a good education.

Life in St. Paul was not especially trying for the Wilkins children. They lived in a predominantly white neighborhood and since public accommodations were not segregated Roy recalls no particular illfeeling between his white playmates and himself. He and his brothers and sister did however attend the all-black St. James A.M.E. Church, where Roy was a boy soprano in the choir. He also attended Whittier Elementary School, where he became manager of the baseball team. And at the Mechanics Arts High School his leanings toward writing found him editing that school's newspaper. After school hours he contributed to his support by working as a golf caddy and dishwasher.

Following high school Roy entered the University of Minnesota to major in sociology. As an undergraduate student he defrayed his expenses by working as a redcap, Pullman car waiter, and meat-packing-house laborer. While working as an editor on the University's *Minnesota Daily,* he became interested in civil rights. Always a keen scholar, he developed his capacities as a public speaker and won a $50 Pillsbury debating prize for a speech on the lynching of two black circus roustabouts in Duluth. It seemed only natural that as a University senior he would become Secretary of the then young and strongly anti-lynching N.A.A.C.P.

But upon graduation from the University in 1923 he left the N.A.A.C.P. to join the staff of *The Kansas City Call,* a black weekly newspaper of which he later became Managing Editor. As a reporter young Wilkins found living conditions for black residents of Kansas City intolerable. The Missouri city was so strictly segregated that many blacks referred to it as "up south." Every facility used by black citizens from hospital to cemetery was separate from and unequal to those used by whites.

What really incensed reporter Wilkins, however, was a local school bond issue that called for nearly one million dollars for an athletic field for a white high school, and less than $30,000 for the remodeling of a factory building for a black elementary school. Wilkins wrote bitter comments on that issue. Moreover, in his weekly column "Talking It Over," he successfully led an attack against a large local bakery that did a lucrative business in the black neighborhood. The bakery, however, hired no black workers. Under Wilkins' attack *The Call* directed a vigorous editorial campaign toward black housewives urging them to boycott the bakery's goods. It wasn't long before the bakery hired black help.

The local branch of the N.A.A.C.P. took a good long look at the bright young journalist and asked him to become its Director. He accepted. Now since every branch of the N.A.A.C.P. was committed to the abolition of racial segregation in its community, the crusading spirit of young Roy Wilkins was just what the organization needed and wanted. In a very short time Wilkins' work came to the attention of the organization's national office in New York City.

The Crisis, a monthly magazine, is the N.A.A.C.P. official organ and W. E. B. DuBois was its dynamic founder and editor during the 1920s. Dr. DuBois wrote to Roy Wilkins offering a job on the magazine's staff. But Wilkins declined, offering in his letter of reply a critical analysis of *The Crisis.* Scholarly Dr. DuBois, appreciative of Roy's sharp mind, showed the letter to Joel E. Spingarn, the N.A.A.C.P.'s President. Later, when the national office was looking about for an assistant to Executive Secretary

Walter White, Mr. Spingarn remembered Roy Wilkins' letter.

It was 1931 when Wilkins resigned from his job as managing editor of *The Kansas City Call* and moved with his wife to New York City. His first major assignment for the N.A.A.C.P. was a stinger. It was as if the organization was saying to the brash young man, "All right, let's *see* how good you are!"

For several years the Mississippi River, overflowing its banks, had destroyed valuable property. Finally the U. S. Government set up its Mississippi River Control Project, designed to strengthen the levees. It wasn't long before complaints of harsh race discrimination began to come out of the area. White workers, it was alleged, were earning more than blacks for the same labor. Bone-chilling tales of how blacks were brutalized by police were whispered about. Reports of how blacks were earning as little as ten cents an hour and how top pay of $2.50 a day went to that rarest of rare workers, the black caterpillar driver. The N.A.A.C.P. wanted a firsthand report and it dispatched two black reporters to Mississippi to get it. Along with Roy Wilkins they sent the brilliant journalist George S. Schuyler.

The pair set out from New York City by train looking as any two well-groomed reporters should look. When they arrived in Memphis, Tennessee, however, they purchased overalls and shoes like those worn by southern laborers. In their disguise they parted company in Memphis with the understanding that they would pose as itinerant laborers seeking work in the camps. They would get their stories, rejoin in Memphis at a given time, and return to New York together.

It was the only way they could hope to accomplish their mission in such hostile territory. Southern political and economic power was rooted in terror and fear. In the previous ten years Mississippi had officially lynched fifty-eight, Louisiana twenty, Arkansas twenty, and Alabama thirteen. The victims were of course black. Mississippi blacks had been lynched for such officially listed "crimes" as "conjuring," "bad reputation," "unknown offense," and "no offense." Such was the deep south atmosphere of the 1920s and '30s.

Wilkins and Schuyler knew the risks they were taking, and all went well until, through an unfortunate mistake, Schuyler was arrested in a Vicksburg, Mississippi, rooming house. It seems that the rooming house landlady, upon learning that a Negro fugitive robber unknown to the neighborhood was at large, assumed that George Schuyler was the wanted man and called the police. The latter, upon learning who Schuyler was and what he was doing in Mississippi, immediately jailed him. After a night of quick thinking and smooth talking Schuyler convinced the police that he had not been a working reporter in Mississippi but in nearby Louisiana. The officers, not sure of what to do in such a case, snarled a warning: "Nigger, you git outta Mississippi as fast as you kin. And don't ever let us ketch you in heah agin!"

Wilkins, more fortunate, ran into no such snags, and though both men got their stories they could not rejoin in Memphis as originally planned. However, in New York their combined report was published by the N.A.A.C.P. in a pamphlet titled *Mississippi River Slavery, 1932*. Distributed among influential officials, it paved the way for reforms instituted in 1933 by Senator Robert F. Wagner of New York.

Wilkins became editor of *The Crisis* in 1934, a responsibility he carried until 1949. In the interim he had much to think and write about. Little was done to enlist young black men in the armed forces as Hitler stormed across Europe. American left-wingers, as Bayard Rustin dis-

covered, whooped it up for black liberation in America—
until Hitler marched on Russia. Then Wilkins, Bayard
Rustin, and other black leaders noted ruefully how the
"comrades" quickly abandoned the black American and
his struggle for what all white Americans took for granted.

When World War II was over nearly a million black
men had seen active war service. Again lynchings went on
the upswing, prompted by white fear and resentment of
black men who had lived and died overseas as *men*. White
resistance to black aspirations at home continued to challenge decency. In 1954, through the excellent legal work
of the N.A.A.C.P. chief counsel, Thurgood Marshall, the
Supreme Court ruled that the nation's school segregation
must end. It appeared that at last a monumental victory
for equality had been won.

But the ruling failed to specify a time for accomplishing that end. Those unwilling to desegregate their schools
blamed the N.A.A.C.P. and its chief attorney Thurgood
Marshall for stirring up trouble. Three years later Little
Rock, Arkansas, showed its brutal ugliness as nine black
children marched to a formerly white school under armed
Federal guard to the cadence of white adult screams and
curses. Inside the school white children insulted and ter-
rorized the newly arrived black children. Again irate
whites charged the Supreme Court, the N.A.A.C.P., and
Mrs. Daisy Bates of Little Rock with "creating more
trouble."

Roy Wilkins was in complete command of the N.A.A.-
C.P., having succeeded Walter White, who died in 1955.
Since he was chief, criticism aimed at the organization
went right to his desk. His patience in the face of continued official dallying with the rights of black people began to draw fire from other black leaders. A few of whom
were N.A.A.C.P. local affiliates. The opposition cried that
the masses of black people were not impressed by lengthy

legal battles ending in paper decrees and little else. Others contended that black people could scarcely hope for anything beneficial to them from a "white-controlled" organization. Why, they demanded, was the N.A.A.C.P. less successful than the Montgomery movement led by Dr. King?

Wilkins replied that because Montgomery, Alabama's black citizens formed 70 per cent of that city's bus riders their boycott against the bus line was bound to be successful. He further declared that in most American cities the low ratio of blacks to whites gives whites all the economic, political, and physical power. Winning huge numbers of whites to the black man's side, he contended, is the only chance blacks have of winning any significant battles.

Such was the Wilkins approach in the 1950s. It has not undergone any major revisions since. Because with Martin Luther King, Jr., he endorsed the Gandhian methods for dealing with injustice, Wilkins joined the 1956 Montgomery protest demonstration. And they were joined by Ralph J. Bunche, Kenneth Clark, James Farmer, Bayard Rustin, Ruby Hurley, and Ella Baker, who shared their belief in the nonviolent direct action protest. But pernicious and ravishing disease that it is, racial persecution did not retreat or abate in the presence of peaceful protest. Actually it began to intensify as bigoted whites saw in the protests what they considered a threat to their security. White reaction among bigots therefore was often violent. And it was answered by violence in black communities throughout America during the early 1960s. Roy Wilkins responded to it in his own way.

The murder of Medgar Evers at the doorway of his home evoked the quiet Wilkins anger. He and the scholarly young Mississippi N.A.A.C.P. field worker had only days before been arrested in Jackson, because they had picketed a department store that hired no black sales clerks. So Wilkins angrily and sadly joined Martin Luther King, Jr., in leading a march of Evers' mourners in the Mississippi capital city. And, as has been stated, he was a principal participant in the March on Washington. When, just prior to that vast demonstration, someone asked him what he was seeking as a marcher, Wilkins replied, "Equality is the basic goal of the N.A.A.C.P. and of the entire civil rights movement . . . The barriers which set the Negro apart from his fellow Americans must be leveled before substantial and lasting progress can be made toward real equality."

Obviously Wilkins was not convinced two years later in 1965 that such real equality had been achieved. The burning and pillaging in the California ghetto called Watts, moved him to open his column in *The New York Post* (August 22) with these words:

"The Los Angeles rioting last week has multiple roots running deep in the Negro community and deeper into the white community. The blind craziness of the roving Negro mobs was created by the blind craziness of white people over at least the past hundred years. The basic problem in 1865 was the making of men and citizens out of slaves who had been mere property. The nation met that problem by continuing a slave system—unlabeled— and slave psychology into the mid-twentieth century."

Wilkins' concluding statements are no less forthright:

"A solution of the problem of 1865 will elude the nation as long as the white community keeps the hidden and the visible screws on Negroes. And we will have ghetto upheavals until the Negro community itself, through the channels that organized societies have fashioned since tribal beginnings, takes firm charge of its destiny. Not its destiny vis-à-vis a cop on the beat, but its destiny in the world of adults. The Negro race, if only for its own self-respect, cannot abdicate to gangs of plundering punks."

Two years and many riots later Wilkins again wrote in the *New York Post*, July 8, 1967:

"Buffalo, N.Y., has chosen to call its upheaval a "rampage" rather than a riot, but whatever the label, a complicated, sensitive, often ugly and extremely difficult interracial problem is again presented.

"It is not a simple thing (as many white people argue) like Negroes "behaving themselves" and "observing law and order." It is not a simple thing (as many Negroes argue) like white people "giving us jobs and treating us fairly."

"No good can come of talk by white people of "cracking down," just as no good can come of physical attacks by Negroes on white passers-by. Beating up a white Joe Jones and his wife does not frighten whites, but only stiffens opposition to Negro demands. Indiscriminate cracking down by police does not frighten Negroes: it merely spurs the waging and condoning of guerrilla counter-resistance."

A balanced Roy Wilkins was applying reason to a situation created by a lack of reason. At the same time he felt justified in criticizing Martin Luther King, Jr.'s linking of the war in Vietnam to the civil rights struggle of black Americans. King had said in a speech in April 4, 1967, that black Americans were "dying in disproportionate numbers in Vietnam. A nation that continues year after year to spend more money on military defense than on programs of social uplift is approaching spiritual death." The nation's press attacked the statement and Wilkins went along with the press.

Divergent as were the views of Wilkins and King on that issue, their disagreement was all but inundated in the swells of a fresh and strident young voice demanding and getting public attention. The voice was that of twenty-six-year-old Stokely Carmichael, and it shouted (though it had by no means coined) the phrase *"Black Power!"* Roy Wilkins listened carefully before responding.

Carmichael, a brilliant young alumnus of one of the nation's finest high schools (New York City's Bronx High School of Science) was a provocative and a persuasive public speaker. Since he was handsome and personable, his appeal to youth, especially black youth, was phenomenal. Forty years separated Wilkins and Carmichael. Yet they were bound together by the same racism and drew the delicately balanced rapier thrusts of the former and the boisterous roundhouse battle-axe style of the latter. Those news reporters anxious to report to the nation and the world how hopelessly split black leadership was, rushed to Wilkins for a story. What did he think of Carmichael and those new power shoutings of his?

The first thing Wilkins said was that there was nothing new in it, that black people had been seeking the same goals for the past seventy-five years. He added that, in spite of Stokely's insistence that there has been no black progress, black Americans do hold jobs denied them in years past, and that there are statistics to prove it. Furthermore, he added, President Lyndon B. Johnson, of whom Carmichael thought very little, had actually done more for civil rights than any other President before him. That too, he asserted, was a matter of official record.

Wilkins, in praise of Carmichael and other young black militants, has said this:

"I admire them in so many ways. They've brought so many kinds of things into the movement; an honesty, a daring boldness, a lack of fear that's refreshing—sometimes topped with rudeness and brashness, but there you are. Their good qualities have been invaluable in stimulating the older Negroes. I'm free to admit that Stokely, by slogans and sloganizing, has aroused the people. These boys may have oversimplified, but they've done good work.

"*But* they either know nothing about or they distort the history of their own struggle. There's room in civil rights for their brains, their impatience, their innovations, their energy. Especially their tremendous energy. Now if we could only harness it . . . Sometimes I think we need the injection of their virus into the dead community. I don't dismiss them, I don't sneer at them. It's just that I sometimes sneer at what they say."

The Wilkins pat on the back for the youthful opposition outside his organization does not mean he hesitates to deal firmly with young dissenters within the group. During its 1968 Annual Convention the disruptive actions of six hundred youthful N.A.A.C.P. delegates made news all over the country. They made it clearly known that they had little faith in the older leadership, which they declared to be outdated and irrelevant to their problems.

However, during the Annual Convention in Jackson, Mississippi, the following year, the N.A.A.C.P. formally announced to the delegates that the young dissidents had undergone a complete change of heart. And not a single youthful denial was heard. Roy Wilkins, the seasoned warrior, obviously has a knack for handling family squabbles quietly and effectively. Most important, he knows the art of maintaining the strength of organizational unity.

Now what of the N.A.A.C.P. itself—its general makeup and character? Well, it is the nation's oldest and richest civil rights organization. Founded in 1909 at the instigation of Mary White Ovington, an affluent social worker, its present membership of nearly half a million is predominantly black. The N.A.A.C.P. income for 1968 exceeded three million dollars, more than half of which came from foundations—Ford, Rockefeller, and Carnegie —and from other philanthropists. The rest of its money came from its 90 per cent black membership.

That membership includes the professional, semiprofessional, and poor laboring classes. There are thirteen hundred branches of record, and branch officials are people with secure incomes. Its National Board of Directors, which numbers about sixty, consists of black and white, middle-aged, and financially stable.

The tone of the N.A.A.C.P. from top to bottom is solid, staid, and conservative. This is quickly seen when one visits its national headquarters in New York, whose Broadway offices are furnished as are those of any efficiently run white business firm. Indeed, its very appearance reflects the Wilkins—and the traditional N.A.A.C.P.—philosophy of cooperation with the white establishment. It seems hardly likely that the organization as it is presently run by Wilkins will curry the establishment's disfavor. Still enduring tranquility for the man who heads it is an elusive quality.

For one thing, there is the Wilkins awareness of the articulate young and not so young who do not feel his methods suit the demands of the day. He knows, for instance, there are many sober and thoughtful American patriots among the anti-Vietnam demonstrators. Since he disassociated his organization and its aims from the war in Vietnam, many disturbing facts about Vietnam have been discovered. The most disturbing, to the American conscience, are the ugly and documented instances of the needless murder of defenseless Vietnamese old men, women, and children by American soldiers.

Thanks to good reporting, it has been learned that black and white G.I.'s alike had a share in the incidents. Wilkins, the former newsman who exposed slum conditions and inequities in Kansas City, and who condemned black ghetto hooligans, knows this. And it is not likely that his honest reporter's instincts have forsaken him.

When President Nixon took office, Wilkins, a Democrat, characteristically, hoped for the best in the area of civil rights. After all, he reasoned, it was only fair that black citizens give the new President a chance to perform. But the Nixon administration quickly forced Clifford Alexander, able black chairman of the Equal Employment Opportunity Commission, out of his job. Wilkins was not pleased.

Four months later Judge Clement F. Haynsworth, Jr., was named by the new President to the U. S. Supreme Court. Wilkins was outraged. Judge Haynsworth, a South Carolina jurist, had voted for racial segregation in at least four cases. And Wilkins had the evidence to support his claim. Recalling another judge of North Carolina, John J. Parker, who was defeated by N.A.A.C.P. action in 1930, Wilkins did what came naturally. He fought for the rejection of Judge Haynsworth, and he won.

Meanwhile, after fifteen years of delaying tactics, the President did uphold the Supreme Court's ruling that Mississippi school desegregation must proceed without further delay. But southern old-guard opposition began its usual fight to preserve segregation, and Wilkins finds himself about to engage in a repeat of an old legal battle. The taunts of the militants of the 1950s that legal paper decrees are worthless are again being repeated by the militants of 1970.

Wilkins, the alert man, hears those taunts. Wilkins, the intelligent and sensitive man, cannot help but be disturbed by them. So he is faced with the herculean task of leading the nation's most prestigious civil rights organization through a period of awesome turbulence. And in so doing he must be allowed the freedom to do it in his own way.

Just what will eventually and finally take place in American civil rights and what part Roy Wilkins will finally have in it will be decided by history. He already has a prominent place in the struggle, for his accomplishments to date are on the record and they are considerable. He has been human and he has been dedicated in the performance of the assignment he has undertaken. Only a man of steely intelligence, skill, and a large measure of personal courage can hope to accomplish it. And Roy Wilkins gives no evidence of wanting to give up the fight.

Thurgood Marshall

IT WAS A horrible incident and it erupted in Springfield, Ohio, in the year 1908 on a humid August day. A nondescript but comely woman, fearful that her extramarital affair would be exposed, declared she had been raped. Her attacker, she sobbed, was a black man. Within minutes a mob of men assembled and seized a black man who happened to be in the vicinity of the woman's home.

Quick police action, however, saved the man—who, it developed, had never seen the woman—from a savage lynching. But the unsated passions of the mob, intensified by frustration, were aflame and out of control. Within a short time other frenzied mobs joined the first and hustled into Springfield's black community. So swift and destructive were they that five thousand militiamen had to be called into Springfield from nearby Decatur. When some semblance of order was restored two black men had been lynched. One of them was eighty-four years old. Four white men lost their lives, over seventy persons sustained injuries, and black owned and occupied dwellings were destroyed by fire. And as had been true in similar attacks occurring in the south no effort was made to find and punish those who had started the trouble.

Decent white Americans, believing that such hatred existed only in the south, were horrified by the Springfield atrocity. One of them was the distinguished writer William English Walling, who went to Springfield and wrote on what he found there. His story, titled "Race War in the North," and published in *The Independent,* was read in New York by Mary White Ovington, a well-to-do social worker. Miss Ovington was outraged.

Losing no time, she called together writer Walling, Dr. Henry Moskowitz, and Oswald Garrison Villard, and the four of them decided to call a conference for the following February 12. They would ask Jane Addams, John Dewey, and William Dean Howells to join them. They would also invite members of The Niagara Movement, a group of black intellectuals headed by W. E. B. DuBois, that had been founded five years previously. And together they would press for equal civil rights for all citizens, as well as an end to lynching and race riots.

What followed at that conference was the founding of The National Association for the Advancement of Colored People. The year was 1909. No one, of course, knew that a curly-haired infant boy in Baltimore, Maryland, would later perform a distinguished service for America within the program of that equally infant organization.

The child's parents, William Canfield Marshall and Norma Arica, had named him Thoroughgood, after his grandfather. Later he, himself, was to shorten his name to Thurgood. He was born on July 2, 1908, and until he was nearly five they called him "Goody," largely because he was a timid little fellow who cried a lot.

His father was a steward at the fancy Gibson Island Club on the Chesapeake Bay, and everybody who knew William Marshall knew he was no pushover. He taught his two sons, Aubrey and Thurgood, to fight for their rights when they had to. The boy's mother, a teacher in the

Baltimore schools, was a strict disciplinarian in the classroom and at home as well. It was from her that Thurgood learned to study and to behave himself while he was about it.

The schools Thurgood attended, like those his mother and all black teachers worked in, were strictly segregated. They were old buildings that had been used when the neighborhoods were exclusively white. As the need for more residential space for black families grew they quickly seized what fleeing white families left behind. As a matter of course they inherited the well-used neighborhood schools.

One high school only existed for all of Baltimore's black children. For many years it was known simply as "The Colored High School" and it was located on Pennsylvania Avenue next to the Northwestern police station. Only a dark green wooden fence shielded the school's narrow yard from the ground-floor cells of the police station. The small dingy school with slate stairwells had basement toilet facilities, no auditorium, and no gymnasium. A tiny brick-paved yard at the rear of the building served as a recreation area, and that was rendered even smaller by a portable wooden single classroom building crammed into the limited space. School hours began at 8 A.M. and ended at 5 P.M., accommodating two shifts of students.

Thurgood's class of 1925 was the last to be graduated before the high school was relocated in a new building not far from the old one. And Baltimore's old Colored High School proudly took the name of Maryland-born Frederick Douglass, the irrepressible slave who became an abolitionist as well as an international orator, writer, and statesman.

At high school gangling, boisterous Thurgood Marshall was known to his classmates as "Legs." A first-rate student in spite of his raucous manner, he excelled in English and history and finished his four-year course in three and a half years. It has been said that he was absent from high school only once and that he was never late. Perhaps so. Without intending to tarnish the luster of such a record it should be reported that Uncle Cyrus Marshall was the high school's freshman math teacher and his constant presence in the school just *may* have encouraged Thurgood to get there so regularly and so promptly.

While he was in high school, Thurgood thought he would want to be a physician. His father, however, wanted him to study law, but William Marshall was too shrewd to order Thurgood, along with four of his high school classmates, went on to nearby Lincoln University for black students in Oxford, Pennsylvania.

Lincoln, an all men's school for black American and African students, can be justly proud of its many nationally and internationally distinguished graduates. The boys, proud of their school's academic tradition, were equally proud of its masculine image. So no one would consider Lincoln men effete, they, to a man, established reputations for being rough and ready. A fitting expression used by outsiders in describing a Lincoln man was, "He hath no couth." And Lincoln University was the perfect setting for the uninhibited personality of young Thurgood Marshall.

It wasn't surprising, therefore, that Thurgood, loud and rough as any of them, was expelled in his sophomore year for excessive hazing of freshmen. But the faculty soon reversed its decision, and he went back to become an outstanding member of the debating team, and to be grad-unceremoniously his son to be a lawyer. He had first to prime the boy. And he did that by engaging Thurgood in debates and arguments designed to develop in his son a logical and analytical mode of thought and expression. Upon graduation from high school both Marshall boys, stimulated by their parents, wanted further education.

uated with a "B" average. He had meanwhile met, wooed, and married a most attractive University of Pennsylvania coed, Miss Vivian ("Buster") Burey.

Young Thurgood Marshall, with a Bachelor of Arts degree and a wife, knew he needed more training for whatever he was going to pursue as his life's work, though he was not yet completely sure of what it was.

During the summer he did odd jobs, even trying his luck as an insurance salesman. Then, as he began to turn the possibilities over in his mind and to re-engage his father in debate, he knew. He was meant to be a lawyer. Wise old William Marshall had been conditioning his son for it all along.

First choice was the Law School at the University of Maryland, but Thurgood Marshall was rejected because of his color. When he entered Howard University's Law School in Washington, D.C., he made two resolutions. First, he was through clowning and kidding around. He would study hard and be the best lawyer he could possibly be. Second, when he became a lawyer he'd do something about cracking that color line at the University of Maryland.

At Howard, Thurgood came under the tutelage of one of America's great law teachers, Charles Houston. "Charley Houston," as intimates knew him, was determined as a black man that Howard's second-rate Law School would rank with the finest. He knew that only the finest kind of legal training would enable its young black graduates to fight segregation in the courts successfully. As Dean of the Law School, Houston dedicated himself to that end.

Thurgood idolized Houston. When he was graduated in 1933 he led his class and he started out in Maryland to argue civil rights cases. The way was rough, for those were depression days, and the clients whom he represented had no money. Still, he had some things going for him. For one thing, his secretaries adored him. Because they be-

Malcolm X
Drawing by Elton C. Fax

Bayard Rustin

Sam Reiss

Whitney M. Young, Jr.

Coretta Scott King

Roy Wilkins

Fabian Bachrach

Thurgood Marshall

Fannie Lou Hamer
Drawing by Elton C. Fax

Floyd B. McKissick

Charles Evers

Carl B. Stokes

Richard Gordon Hatcher

Edward W. Brooke

Ruby Dee

Ed James

Kenneth Bancroft Clark

lieved in what he was doing they stuck with him even
when he was unable to pay them the full amount of their
meager salaries. Sometimes they even treated him to lunch
when they knew he had no money. Then a case came to
his attention—a case so familiar as to jerk him upright at
his desk.

A young black man, Donald Murray, having been
denied admittance to the Law School of the University of
Maryland, had come to Thurgood for help. Ha! So he
would have his old adversary in court much sooner then
he had thought. What could be more perfect? This is what
he had dared not hope for so early in his career. With the
guidance and help of his friend and former mentor, Charley Houston, Thurgood Marshall broke the color bar at
the University of Maryland.

When Dean Houston left Howard University in 1935
to become chief N.A.A.C.P. counsel in New York City he
sent for young Marshall to join him. Thurgood, the deadly
serious young lawyer, was still the earthy and unaffected
human being. In his easy-going and quite irreverent manner he broke through the stiff, cold formality that per-
vaded the organization's home office. His starting salary,
a modest $2,400 a year, was, as he put it, no reason for
him or for anyone else at the N.A.A.C.P. to "put on airs."

Houston resigned in 1938 to enter private law practice
and Thurgood Marshall became the Director-Counsel of
the N.A.A.C.P.'s Legal Defense and Educational Fund.
Marshall, meanwhile, had developed his philosophy of
what legal equality meant to black Americans. It did not
satisfy him merely to realize that a few gains were being
made by a few individuals, for he knew that most such
gains were guaranteed by the Constitution anyway.

When someone would say, "But look how *far* the Negro has come in the last ten years," Thurgood had an
answer. "What you've got to do," he'd reply, "is to mea-

sure where they are in relation to white people." In this he is paraphrased by Whitney Young, when Young says that the back wheels of the car can't possibly catch up to the front wheels if they travel at the same speed. Marshall held that the Fourteenth Amendment was adopted so that the black ex-slave could move into full-fledged American citizenship. And he was determined that the U. S. Supreme Court would honor that truth in its review of cases involving the Fourteenth Amendment.

The N.A.A.C.P. sent him out to defend clients in the most hostile areas of the deep south and there he mastered the art of battleground survival. He was menaced and threatened by a gun-wielding Mississippian and stopped numerous times in Tennessee by police anxious to pin charges of law violations on him. At the end of the tour he had come to the conclusion that every N.A.A.C.P. representative in the south lives constantly in the shadow of violent death. "I don't believe I could take it for a week," he declared.

Within very recent years, when young activists, unaware of past performances in civil rights, challenged Thurgood Marshall to "go south with the freedom marchers," he said simply, "I've already been. I was there when your father was afraid to be caught out on southern streets after dark." The youngsters were stunned. It was obvious some of them thought the graying jurist was joking, for many believed black participation in civil rights protests began only when they heard of them in the early 1960s.

One of the difficult obstacles for Marshall to overcome in seeking equal school opportunities in the south was the south's insistence that while its schools were separate they were of equal quality. This clearly was not true. Most all-white schools offered facilities to white children that did not exist in black schools. And where seemingly similar facilities existed they proved under close inspection to be invariably inferior in the black schools. Proving this was a drawn-out and costly legal procedure. Besides, by his own admission, Marshall and his staff didn't yet know enough to win such cases.

A break in southern tradition did, however, occur as he tried to enroll Herman Sweatt in the Law School at the University of Texas. The University, seeking to block Sweatt's enrollment, tried to set up a law school in Texas for black students. But white students themselves, more than two hundred of them, set up a branch of the N.A.A.-C.P. on campus. Their purpose was to collect enough money to pay the legal costs of fighting the University's stand. Marshall won the case in 1950. Almost simultaneously he won a similar case at Oklahoma State University. And within a year more than a thousand black students entered southern university graduate schools.

In 1951, investigating charges that black G.I.'s were being discriminated against by the Far Eastern Command, Thurgood went on an investigating tour of Korea. His work took him to the front lines, where he learned what it is like to be under sniper fire. Before returning home he heard the cases of and substantially aided twenty-two enlisted men who had received unusually harsh sentences under court-martial.

Back in America he resumed his efforts to enforce the "equal protection clause" of the Fourteenth Amendment. He was again going to attack the "separate but equal" doctrine. This time he knew exactly how to do it. The old 1896 Supreme Court decision in the Plessy vs. Ferguson case which supported the separate but equal doctrine had to be overthrown *scientifically.* So Marshall sent Robert Carter, one of his assistants, to talk with psychologist Kenneth B. Clark about the effects of racial segregation on black children.

Dr. Clark, a black professor at New York City College

and whose biography appears later in this book, had previously done enlightening research on the subject. His studies revealed that black children between the ages of three and seven reacted in a uniformly different manner to a pair of brown dolls and a pair of white ones. Except for color the dolls were identical. Yet the majority of the children tested showed a decided preference for the white dolls. Dr. Clark concluded that black children exposed to segregation suffered deep feelings of inferiority. He further concluded that forced segregation *implies* inferiority and that the segregated school is the worst offender.

Using this evidence along with figures showing the gap between monies spent for white and black children's education Marshall carried four suits to the U. S. Supreme Court. The defending states were Kansas, South Carolina, Virginia, and Delaware. And Thurgood Marshall would challenge them with a document prepared by three psychologists and endorsed by thirty-two outstanding social scientists. Its title was "The Effects of Segregation and the Consequences of Desegregation."

The Supreme Court heard the first arguments during October 1952, and it heard final arguments fourteen months later. In the interim Thurgood literally lived up to his name. He and his staff did a *thorough* job of going over every inch and into every cranny of each case. Following a method used by Charley Houston, they conducted mock hearings to find and correct weaknesses in their briefs. After long days of such preparation the Marshall team was ready.

A packed courthouse listened intently as Thurgood calmly delivered his argument. Gone was the rollicking boisterous manner so familiar to friends. Nor was he airily trying to impress with an attitude of the superscholar. His language, clear and simple, was directed to the very vitals of the system of segregation. Here in part, is what he said:

"I got the feeling (from what has been said here) that when you put a white child in a school with a whole lot of colored children, the child would fall apart or something. Everybody knows that is not true. Those same kids in Virginia and South Carolina—and I have seen them do it—they play in the streets together, they play on their farms together, they go down the road together, they separate to go to school, they come out of school and play ball together. They have to be separated in school . . . Why, of all the multitudinous groups of people in this country do you have to single out the Negroes and give them this separate treatment?

"It can't be because of slavery in the past, because there are very few groups in this country that haven't had slavery some place in the history of their groups. It can't be color, because there are Negroes as white as drifted snow, with blue eyes, and they are just as segregated as the colored men. The only thing it can be is an inherent determination that people who were formerly in slavery, regardless of anything else, shall be kept as near that stage as possible. And now is the time, we submit, that this Court should make it clear that that is not what our Constitution stands for."

Eighty-one-year-old John W. Davis presented the case for the opposing side. In the traditionally courtly manner of the old south, Mr. Davis appealed for the preservation of states' rights over Federal authority and particularly over the Fourteenth Amendment. Then both sides rested their cases. It was five months later before Chief Justice Earl Warren handed down the Court's decision, which read in part:

"In the field of public education the doctrine of 'separate

but equal' has no place . . . separate educational facilities are inherently unequal.''

Reaction to the ruling ranged from the jubilant approval of the N.A.A.C.P. and *The New York Herald Tribune* to the bitter condemnation of the south. Marshall was, of course, delighted with the legal victory but he was soberly cautious. When the office staff at N.A.A.C.P. headquarters talked about having a celebration, he had some of his good-natured earthy advice for them. "You fools had better quit that damn rejoicing and get yourselves ready for the battle that lies ahead!" Though he did not know it at that moment, the victorious attorney had reason to be reserved and sober.

With no prior warning the Marshall's family physician informed Thurgood that his wife, Buster, had terminal cancer. The blow was almost too much to bear and during the final weeks of her illness Thurgood sought the seclusion of their home.

Three months later, when the Supreme Court finally and formally announced its decision, it directed the states to end school segregation "with all deliberate speed." But the decision was far from flawless. There was no fixed time schedule for compliance. Moreover, the Court did not this time endorse the recommendations of the social scientists, and its final decision carried an air of uneasy vagueness. Then in 1957 came the first explosive reaction. Arkansas, led by its Governor Orville Faubus, refused to recognize the new law.

It took the force of Federal Marshals and troops to lead nine black children through a mob of screaming hostile white adults to Little Rock's Central High School. During the continued legal squabbling that ensued, President Eisenhower at a Washington news conference advised a slowdown in school integration. That, added to the absence of any positive deadline on school desegregation, made prompt compliance with the new law impossible. Marshall's courtroom victory was not getting the support it had earned.

But Thurgood continued to win civil rights cases (twenty-nine out of thirty-two in the Supreme Court) and he was offered handsome inducements to enter private practice. Though he was now the nation's leading constitutional lawyer, he elected to remain with the N.A.A.-C.P.

His home life was happy again, for he had married pretty Cecilia Suyat, who had been employed as a secretary in the national office of the N.A.A.C.P. Hawaiian-born "Cissy," as she is called, had been a student at the Business School of Columbia University. Her traditional Oriental charm, with its accent on pleasing the man of her choice, had proved to be just what Thurgood needed. He had been tasting a great deal of the bitter along with the sweet and he found the bitter easier to swallow with Cissy and their two sons, Thurgood Jr. and John close by. Life for the Marshalls was growing increasingly brighter.

In 1961 President John F. Kennedy offered Thurgood a Federal judgeship in the United States Circuit Court of Appeals. Thurgood had always avoided accepting "political jobs," but he felt that now was the time to step in another direction. His staff was certainly able to carry on without him, and he agreed to have the President put his nomination before Congress. His supporters were numerous and distinguished, but those opposed to his getting the appointment were in a position to delay it. Headed by Mississippi's Senator James O. Eastland, the opposition tried to link the black nominee with Communism.

Marshall was quizzed by opposing Senators as though he were a delinquent truant seeking to become the superintendent of schools. There was a great deal of bickering involving hard-core southern Democratic Senators and

New York's Republican Senators, Keating and Javits. But one year later Marshall's confirmation was assured by a vote of fifty-six to sixteen. It was clear that the opposition was expressing its sentiments toward anything or anyone who challenged the doctrine of white supremacy.

In his new job Thurgood had to become acquainted with the special facets of law required of him and he went back to his books to get them. He served four productive years on the Federal bench when another call came from another President. In the summer of 1965 Lyndon Baines Johnson was looking for a Solicitor General and he wanted Judge Marshall for the job.

Thurgood thought about it. The new offer of $28,000 a year paid less than his permanent Federal judgeship. But the permanency of that judgeship depended upon the pleasure of the President. The new job would force him and his new wife and children to leave New York City and resettle in Washington. It meant also that as Solicitor General he would occupy the number three place in the Department of Justice. After considering the negatives and positives, Thurgood realized that he would accept. One does not refuse the President's offer. There was the expected southern opposition to the appointment, but this time Senate confirmation was swift.

Marshall's new staff consisted of ten lawyers. Because of the Solicitor General's position, as the government's chief appellate lawyer, the nine judges of the U. S. Supreme Court would listen respectfully to him. The Solicitor General performs vital legal services for the nation. It is his office that decides what cases to appeal to the Supreme Court, what arguments to make, what points to concede. It has to deal especially with confessions extracted by the police from a prisoner; and the right of the prisoner to legal counsel *at police headquarters*. In short, the Solicitor General must recognize that the guilty man's rights are just as inviolate as those of the innocent.

The Solicitor General may or may not dress formally in court. Marshall, the nation's thirty-third and the nation's first black Solicitor General, decided that he would go along with the traditional striped trousers, black shoes, and cutaway coat. Friends and well-wishers, noting his legal advancement, reminded him that his next move would be to the United States Supreme Court. "Many Solicitors General have gone on to the Supreme Court," they assured him. Reverting to his familiar homespun wit, Thurgood usually replied, "Yeah, and a heck of a lot of 'em *haven't!*"

The year 1965 was a severely challenging one for those engaged in the civil rights movement. President Johnson, like his immediate predecessors, had to make a number of meaningful decisions if the nation was to avoid anarchy. And President Johnson was under critical scrutiny. Could a southerner, a man born and reared in racially segregated Texas, rise nobly to the demands of the nation's highest office? After all, President Eisenhower had failed to take a firm stand until forced by violent mobs to protect not only the rights but the *lives* of black school children in Arkansas. In the face of that did black Americans dare *hope* for more from a southerner? Many Americans wondered. None had been more watchful than Thurgood Marshall.

The year had begun ominously with the February slaying in New York of Malcolm X. During the same month Mississippi's U. S. District Judge, W. Harold Cox, dismissed an indictment against seventeen men implicated in the murder of three young civil rights workers—black James Chaney and white Mickey Schwerner and Andy Goodman. In addition, Alabama's Governor Wallace, an arch-segregationist, had requested a White House appointment to discuss his views of racial strife in his state.

For three hours he and President Johnson talked. Meanwhile, black leadership waited apprehensively to see what the Chief Executive would say to the nation in a televised news conference that followed. With Governor Wallace plainly visible in the background, here in part is what they heard their President say:

"Last Sunday a group of Negro Americans in Selma, Alabama, attempted peacefully to protest the denial of the most basic political right of all—the right to vote. They were attacked and some brutally beaten . . . What happened in Selma was an American Tragedy . . . I have made clear, whether the Governor agrees or not, that law and order will prevail in Alabama, that the people's rights to peacefully assemble will be preserved, and that their Constitutional rights will be protected.

Two nights later, on March 15, at a rare joint night session of Congress the nation, through the medium of television, again heard Mr. Johnson call for the voting rights of black citizens. And on March 17 he sent a strong voting rights bill to Congress. In less than ten days the President was again before television cameras denouncing the Ku Klux Klan:

"I have fought them all my life because I believe them to threaten the peace of every community where they exist. I shall continue to fight them because I know their loyalty is not to the United States of America, but instead to a hooded society of bigots."

Mr. Johnson appealed to Klansmen to "get out of the Ku Klux Klan and return to a decent society before it is too late." On April 29, U. S. Commissioner of Education Francis Keppel announced that all of the nation's twenty-seven thousand public school districts would have to desegregate all public schools. And it was to be done by the beginning of the 1967 fall school term, starting in September of 1965.

Black civil rights leaders were impressed by the Texas President, who, in their view, had done more on civil rights in a short time than all his predecessors. They did not blame Mr. Johnson for the failure of an Alabama jury to punish the accused slayers of Mrs. Viola Liuzzo, a white civil rights activist from Detroit. Nor did they blame him for the Los Angeles rioting at Watts in which thirty-five died and damage was estimated at $200 million.

Indeed, black leadership at large was not at all surprised when President Johnson named Thurgood Marshall to the United States Supreme Court. Actually, it is quite likely that Marshall, himself, was not surprised, for though he was too wise to take the appointment for granted, he had grown to admire the tall Texan. He had seen and known many who had done less in the effort to rid the nation of its racist sickness.

In announcing his nomination of Solicitor General Marshall to newsmen on June 13, 1967, the President said of Thurgood Marshall:

"I believe he has already earned his place in history. But I think it will be greatly enhanced by his service on the Court . . . it is the right thing to do, the right time to do it, the right man, and the right place."

Marshall accepted his honors with dignity and went to work at once. A measure of his sense of legal fair play was to be seen in his ruling on October 27, 1969, in the case of the Reverend James F. Groppi. Father Groppi, a white Roman Catholic priest of Milwaukee, had become well known for his unrelenting fight against his city's brand of northern segregation. On October 17, 1969, after many months of protesting racial injustice, Father Groppi was jailed for violating probation by taking part in a Milwaukee demonstration. Justice Marshall reviewed the facts and ruled that the priest was entitled to freedom on bail until the Supreme Court finally ruled in his case. And Father Groppi was promptly released from the House of Correction to await that decision. There is a bit of irony in the fact that the right of a white man, in this case Father Groppi, to justice in the nation's highest court would be upheld by the great-grandson of a black slave. At the same time, it seems quite proper. Who could be expected to be more sensitive to the denial of any man's freedom than a man of the training and the experience of Justice Thurgood Marshall?

Floyd B. McKissick

W<small>HEN</small> T<small>HURGOOD</small> M<small>ARSHALL</small> was attacking segregation in southern colleges and universities during the 1940s, one of the targets was the University of North Carolina. A young black North Carolinian, a veteran of World War II, had applied for admission to the University's Law School. They turned him down cold. The young man was fully eligible. As a citizen of the state and as an academically prepared student he qualified. But the University of North Carolina wasn't budging for Floyd McKissick even with the legal staff of the N.A.A.C.P. behind him.

Still, young McKissick *did* get into that Law School and, more than that, he was to become one of America's ranking lawyers and civil rights activists. That encounter with bigotry at the famous North Carolina University was by no means Floyd's first. Nor was it to be his last. He recalls that he was only four years old when his attractive young aunt took him for a trolley ride in his native Asheville, North Carolina.

Riding the trolley is an exciting experience for small boys. They enjoy watching the motorman reverse the position of the trolley pole. The flying sparks and the blinking of the lights as the pole and overhead wire make contact fascinate them. And when the trolley is in motion all want to crowd as close to the motorman as he will let them get.

Floyd, aglow with excitement, tore away from his aunt, who had taken a seat in the rear of the segregated car, and ran up front to join the knot of white children near the motorman. The motorman glancing about and, spying Floyd, scowled.

"What are you doing up here, nigger boy?" he growled. "Git your black behind to the other end of the car where you belong. I don't see why your mammy don't teach you some manners—butting in where you ain't wanted! *Git back there, boy!*"

The angry voice and the ugly scowl frightened little Floyd. He ran crying toward his aunt, who was already on her feet with arms outstretched. She took the little fellow and she held him close as she stroked him and soothed him with soft words. A few moments later she and Floyd left that trolley and walked home. Today, forty-five years later, Floyd McKissick has not forgotten that episode.

The only boy in a family of four children, Floyd was born in Asheville, North Carolina, on March 9, 1922, to Ernest and Magnolia Esther Thompson McKissick. Ernest McKissick, a veteran of World War I, was able through a government payment to buy a small home for his family. He and his wife completed Livingstone Normal School and each of their four children received a college education. Floyd's mother, eligible to teach, chose instead to work as a seamstress because it paid more than teaching. He recalls:

"My folks were poor, respectable, church-going people. I went through those rough depression years as a child but at a knowledgeable age where I could see and understand hard times."

So young Floyd worked at every conceivable job a boy could do.

He learned early that a wagon could be a useful thing to a boy. And since "store-bought" wagons were out of the question for the poor, Floyd made his own. Old lumber from torn-down houses, wooden boxes, wheels, nails and screws—the wood properly cut and put together—produced a good wagon. Floyd became an expert wagonmaker, often turning them out for others in his community.

With his wagon Floyd was able to sell blocks of ice during the summer to housewives who had no refrigerators. When the weather was hot he could expect to sell enough ice to clear a dollar each day. In addition, he sold black weekly newspapers, gaining thereby not only a little money but a knowledge from the papers of what was happening in America's black communities.

But the summers were also fun. There was baseball, for instance. And there was that formidable gang of black kids who lived over the hill in a section of Asheville called "The Hollow." It was strictly rough-and-tumble in The Hollow and Floyd's team had to be prepared for a knock-down and drag-out session each time they played ball there.

"Man," he recalls, "if around the eighth inning we were ahead we had to start getting our equipment together, 'cause we'd have to get up over that hill to get home. We knew we'd better make a fast getaway, 'cause if we won the game we were sure going to lose the fight."

Life at home, though not one of material comfort, was always stimulating to Floyd and his sisters. Patriarchal Grandfather Thompson was an articulate Methodist minister whose sermons could "set any church on fire." Grandfather Thompson was ahead of his time in that he spoke out against racial injustice when it wasn't popular to do so. For a time he lived in the McKissick home where he conducted mock church services and mock courtroom trials with Floyd taking the leading roles. From these the boy learned the principles of ethical human conduct as well as how to present a theme. Then on Sundays, when he went to church and listened to Grandfather Thompson preach, he thought that one day he too would be addressing a throng of people.

Friends from Livingstone College frequently visited their home and engaged the family in lively discussions. Theology, the race question, happenings in Africa, and black business ventures were the diet on which the children's minds were fed. Their modest home was visited also by black business entrepreneurs and scholars whom the children grew to know and respect.

When Floyd failed to do well in school, one teacher, in particular, Miss Lucy Mae Harrison, pulled his ear. "There's no excuse for you, Floyd McKissick, because I know your parents encourage *you* to learn." Floyd recalls not only Miss Harrison and Grandfather Thompson as strong influences in his life. In a quite different way an Asheville policeman played a vital role in shaping his destiny.

Floyd, an ardent Boy Scout, was fourteen the year he and another boy were assigned by a neighborhood adult to steer traffic away from a block roped off for ice skating. Asheville, because of its mountains, has severe winters that provide an abundance of snow and ice. And since the city was strictly segregated the public skating area for black children was located in the heart of their residential section.

As Floyd and his scout partner patrolled the outer edges of the ice rink area a policeman stopped and asked them what they were doing there and why a rope was stretched across the street. Floyd explained there was a skating tournament in progress and that he was doing his Scout's duty of keeping the skaters in bounds. The policeman, infuriated at the young black boy's lack of fear of him, became furious.

"Nigger, don't you talk back to a white man. Your people ought to teach you better manners." With that the officer proceeded to slap Floyd across the face with a pair of heavy gauntlets. As the sharp red reflectors on the gauntlets' cuffs cut into the boy's skin, drawing blood, everyone, children and adults, scurried off screaming. Floyd, knocked to the ground, removed a skate as he was being beaten and lashed out at the man, missing his face by inches. Then to the accompaniment of more screams from the crowd and more blows from the policeman, Floyd was hustled off to the police station.

Someone meanwhile had notified his father of what had happened and he, along with several other black men, rushed to the police station. There they managed to mollify the police and effect Floyd's release pending a court hearing. Neighbors seemed greatly relieved that Floyd was not held in custody. Indeed, they were surprised that the boy had "talked back" to the policeman and were grateful that things seemed to have been smoothed over.

But Floyd McKissick was far from grateful. On the contrary, he was amazed and angry to discover that he was being shunned and ostracized by schoolmates and neighbors, who felt he should never have attempted to resist the policeman who beat him. What manner of attitude was *that,* he wondered? And what kind of neighbors were there who could not uphold him in his resistance to police brutality?

He took the business of being a Scout seriously and he earnestly believed that what was good for one Scout was good for all Scouts. But things were not working that way in Asheville.

Floyd knew that he was not an Eagle Scout only because local black Scouts could not take the swimming test because they had no pool to swim in. So as he realized how completely justice was overridden by racism his notions of becoming a minister of the gospel like Grandfather Thompson began to grow dim. Much as he admired Grandfather Thompson and much as he had been encouraged by others to become a preacher, Floyd knew he would have to study law. There would be no peace for him until he could help make the principles of human decency work for *everybody*. Moreover, he had observed that a knowledge of law combined with business activity gave a man independence.

Always a good student, Floyd was offered two scholarships upon graduation from high school. Both were to small struggling black colleges in North Carolina, but Floyd had his mind set on taking a pre-law course at Atlanta's Morehouse College. Friends of his family who visited during the summer of 1939 included a lawyer and his wife. When the eager young Floyd had finished talking with them he was more than ever determined to go to Atlanta.

Floyd had a summer job in the pantry of one of Asheville's plush hotels and he saved all of forty dollars—thirty-five dollars less then he needed to cover his tuition. But the kindly bursar, after good-naturedly chiding Floyd for coming to college with insufficient money, admitted him anyway. Within a few days young McKissick had a job as a campus dining hall waiter, becoming the personal waiter to the eminent Dr. W. E. B. DuBois.

At the end of his first year at Morehouse, Floyd found a job on a tobacco farm, not in his native North Carolina but in Connecticut. With money earned there he was able to pay his bills at Morehouse and to begin his second year with a loan from one of Atlanta's black banks. Then in

1941 the Japanese attack on Pearl Harbor upset everyone's plans.

Floyd was to have been drafted in March 1942. Just one
month prior, however, he left Morehouse and volunteered
in a unit of the Field Artillery. Because of his training he
spent two years as an instructor in one of the Army's lit-
eracy schools, and before going overseas to serve with
America's forces based in Europe he married his boyhood
sweetheart, Evelyn Williams.

Returning to civilian life at the end of 1945, and determined to complete his schooling, he applied for admission
to the University of North Carolina. His application was
completely ignored. For the next year he worked as a
waiter to accumulate money enough to return to Morehouse.

The year was 1947. The Congress of Racial Equality
(CORE) had launched an unusual bus tour which it labeled "The Journey of Reconciliation." CORE at that
time consisted of a small interracial band of pacifists in-
tent upon changing the pattern of segregation on public
carriers. This tour was the first of the Freedom Bus rides,
and the group rode from New York City to four states of
the upper south. One of the passengers on that ride was
Bayard Rustin. He and a white pacifist, George Houser,
had planned the trip.

News of the riders and of the brutal treatment they
received at the hands of the police when they reached
North Carolina struck a familiar and a responsive cord
in Floyd McKissick. Only ten years before he had been
brutalized by Asheville police and he had broken no law
on public carriers. McKissick unhesitatingly joined Rustin and the other riders. And why not? What on earth did
he have to lose? Hadn't he risked life and limb in the
European theater of World War II? And returning home,
hadn't the University of his home state made it plain

they didn't want him as a student? So why shouldn't he ride in a demonstration for freedom?

Determined to continue his education, he re-entered Morehouse College. At the end of a year he had made the Dean's list, and now, with two years of college work, he was eligible for entry into law school. Again he applied to the University of North Carolina, this time with legal backing. The N.A.A.C.P.'s legal staff headed by Thurgood Marshall was behind him now.

While he was waiting for the legal mills to turn in his favor, McKissick entered black North Carolina College, at which the state had hastily set up a law school. This was the south's reply to black demands for a state-supplied education. But it was not an honestly conceived effort, for the quickly thrown-together Law School was not accredited. Moreover, it duplicated the familiar southern "separate but equal" doctrine of education that Thurgood Marshall had so vigorously attacked and discredited before the Supreme Court.

Floyd McKissick led the first group of law pickets against the North Carolina Legislature in an effort to gain accreditation for the school. Their pressure forced the Legislature to release $50,000 to renovate one of the campus buildings. As McKissick puts it today, "We made them create *nearly* equal facilities."

While activity at the newly designed black Law School was taking place, the N.A.A.C.P.'s fight to crack the color line at the all-white University of North Carolina finally brought results. In his senior year at North Carolina College, Floyd McKissick was admitted to the State University Law School at Chapel Hill. Recalling his completion of law school he says, "Technically I finished North Carolina College because I had all my credits and honors *before* I got into the University of North Carolina."

It was 1952 when McKissick, having passed his bar

exam, was admitted to the practice of law in the state of North Carolina. He began a general law practice by joining with a seasoned lawyer in Durham, North Carolina. For three years he wrote briefs, learned a great deal he had never known about his home state, and met many people. When he left to go on his own, Floyd took on civil rights cases starting within his own family. Each of his four children, three girls and a boy, became "firsts" in lowering color bars in Durham's city schools.

"The 1950s were tough years," he recalls. "I represented labor unions and churches and I represented people involved in crimes. At one time they called me 'the queers' lawyer because many of my clients were accused of sex crimes. My clients were all plain poor black folks. No big important black people ever called me to represent them in those early days. That did not happen until the 1960s."

The poverty of his clients notwithstanding, they did provide Floyd the chance to be himself. He handled one of the nation's first welfare cases, and he also handled a case establishing the right of a tenant over the power of a housing authority. Of clients facing the death penalty he says proudly, "I never lost a client to the electric chair or to the gas chamber."

McKissick's early boyhood forays into business ventures and his early realizations of the respect accorded black businessmen in the south were never too far from his thinking. It was to be expected, therefore, that as a young lawyer he would help many local black businesses get a start. He was one of the first black lawyers to handle receiverships, the taking over and administering of property belonging to both black and white North Carolinians. Directing the affairs of the Durham Business and Professional Chain became still another McKissick activity along with work as advisor to the state N.A.A.C.P. Youth groups. But a turning point in his life approached as he became director of the Durham Chapter of The Congress of Racial Equality.

CORE was originally founded in 1942–43. Its purpose was:

". . . to abolish racial discrimination and all resulting inequalities based upon skin color, class, race, religion, or national origin, stressing nonviolent direct action methods, political and economic methods, and community organization."

CORE membership then was composed of high school and college students. In Baltimore, Maryland, their organized interracial groups would quietly enter a restaurant just before lunchtime.

Taking seats, they would give their order, only to be told that blacks could not be served. Without making a fuss they continued to sit in silent protest throughout the lunch hour. Because they occupied all seats, other customers who would have been served could not be seated. Though often abused, beaten, and arrested, their nonviolent approach did secure results. Baltimore's lunch counters abandoned their policy of racial discrimination. The sit-ins spread farther south, where black students were the prime participants. In Nashville, Tennessee, a policeman pulled a slide rule from a boy's pocket with the comment that it was the "damn'est knife I ever seen!"

CORE's most harrowing experience occurred in Anniston, Alabama, in May 1961. The U. S. Supreme Court had just ruled discrimination against traveling passengers in bus terminal restaurants to be illegal and thirteen Freedom Riders set out for Louisiana to test the law. Seven were black. They had some minor trouble along the way and they decided to split into two buses, one a Greyhound, the other a Trailways.

At Anniston, Alabama, a howling mob awaited their arrival. Someone threw an incendiary bomb in the Greyhound bus—and riders scrambled to safety, barely escaping death. The bus was completely destroyed. The Trailways bus hurried on to Birmingham, where it was met by another mob who set upon the riders, beating them at will. Though the U. S. Department of Justice had alerted the Birmingham police to possible violence, not a single officer was there to protect the riders.

Floyd McKissick had discovered a dozen years earlier that *any* antidiscrimination demonstrator, white or black, could expect to be beaten in the south. "It was a question only of the *degree* to which he or she would be roughed up," he asserts. It was March 1966 when CORE appointed McKissick its National Director, succeeding James Farmer.

Three months later James H. Meredith, the first known black student to be graduated from the University of Mississippi, made a startling announcement. He would, he declared, march alone and unarmed through his native Mississippi. He would do it to demonstrate how to conquer old fears and to encourage black Mississippians to vote. Just after Meredith had crossed into Mississippi from Tennessee he was shot from ambush by a white man identified as Aubrey Norvell. First reports that Meredith had been killed were exaggerated, for his wounds fortunately were superficial.

As soon as he heard the news, Floyd McKissick flew to the Memphis hospital where Meredith had been taken for treatment. Martin Luther King, Jr., Stokely Carmichael, and James Lawson were there also, and they jointly issued a proclamation that the march would continue immediately from the spot where Meredith had fallen. For nearly three weeks the march continued through Mississippi. Meredith, himself, recovered sufficiently to rejoin it on the short final leg between Tougaloo College to the state capitol at Jackson. Now the most memorable incident of that March—the thing that newspaper readers heard most about—was a two-word phrase that was to startle an entire nation.

As the marchers reached Grenada, Mississippi, Stokely Carmichael, in his typically youthful and flamboyant manner, began to chant, *"Black Power! Black Power!"* King and other older leaders, aware of the attitude of most whites, disapproved. They did not disapprove of power to black people but at Carmichael's provocative use of the phrase at that time and in that place. They knew well that the average white American's concept of black is that black is ugly and menacing. They knew also that power to most Americans means guns and money. The negative implications of the phrase and how they could be exploited by hostile areas of the news media to discredit black leadership were clear.

Still Carmichael was not to be denied his glorious moments. And as was anticipated by the other ring-wise strategists, the chant *was* picked up and misinterpreted by many news people. Oddly enough, the phrase "Black Power" was neither as new nor as threatening as it was made to appear. Scholarly W. E. B. DuBois had made use of it at the beginning of the century. Richard Wright had titled a book he wrote in 1954 following a visit to Ghana. *Black Power.* And Floyd McKissick had used it at the 1965 CORE convention in Durham, North Carolina. Still America at large was obsessed with a fear of the term.

McKissick grew weary of being asked by radio and TV reporters what it meant. Once on TV he gave this humorous reply:

"Now every living sixth-grade school boy knows what 'black' means. And every sixth-grade school boy knows what 'power' means. Now would you believe that I've had seasoned professors from Harvard and Yale ask me to define Black Power for them?"

When the uproarious laughter subsided he cited his six-

point program for Black Power and Self-Determination as
he had developed it for CORE. Black Power meant: (1)
Economic Power; (2) Political Power; (3) Improved
Self-Image; (4) The Development of Black Leadership;
(5) The Enforcement of Federal Laws; (6) Mobilization
of Black Consumers.

When McKissick took over the top position at CORE
the organization was more than four million dollars in
debt. Bringing his combined legal and business experience to the job, he raised more than three million dollars
in his two-and-a-half years at CORE. It was during the
Meredith Mississippi March that McKissick received an
invitation to join a Citizens Mission to Cambodia. As he
recalls it, the timing could not have been less opportune.
Under constant pressure to give the public a more complete
and accurate interpretation of Black Power than it was
getting from the popular press, he had little time to go
overseas. Besides, the nation's black ghettos were beginning to crackle and explode as the discomforts of summer
descended upon them. It was Floyd's feeling that he should
be as close as possible to the action on the home front.

Still, the more he thought of the invitation the more
he could see its relationship to the work he was engaged in
at home. There on Cambodia's borders lurked the constant
danger of a spill-over of the war in Vietnam and what
that could mean to thousands of innocent civilians. Floyd
McKissick saw that the Southeast Asians, defenseless
against modern western weaponry, shared much in common with similarly placed Africans, Latins, and Afro-
Americans. He would accept the invitation.

Others in the group were author Kay Boyle, Rabbi
Israel Dresner, Donald Duncan of *Ramparts* magazine,
Russell Johnson, a Quaker, and Norman Eisner. A CBS-
TV camera team of correspondent William Stout and
photographer Ed Steinhart completed the mission. Their

purpose was to have a firsthand look at what was happening and to share their findings with fellow Americans back home. Here is a sample comment made by McKissick about that trip:

"I was not prepared for what I was to find in Cambodia. I was not prepared to see the seared and mangled bodies of tiny children—destroyed by American napalm. I was not prepared to witness the utter destruction of a cruel and senseless war . . . I shall continue to oppose the criminal neglect shown our own domestic program and the massive diversion of funds to finance this monstrous war. I shall continue to oppose the cynical use of American black people in the execution of a racist foreign policy which is merely an extension of the ever-present racism here at home."

McKissick was quite obviously in agreement with Martin Luther King, Jr., who linked the Vietnam war with the civil rights struggle when it wasn't popular to do so. In this, both leaders were controversial and eagerly sought as public speakers.

Offers to appear on T.V. panel discussion shows and as a college campus speaker came to McKissick via the CORE national headquarters. Seeing and hearing him became a memorable experience, for he was never dull and he was often painfully funny. With directness and simplicity, underlined by a Carolina mountain accent, he became a master at telling it exactly as it really is. When someone at a college forum once mentioned Lincoln and slavery, McKissick's response was one of swift and deadly wit:

"Lincoln? Lincoln did not free the slaves at all. With all his good intentions, the only thing Abraham Lincoln did was to *fire* the slaves. That was the only time in history that you ever had full employment—when man was enslaved. And when I hear people now say, 'What we need is jobs and full employment,' I say, 'Oh hell, I remember what happened the *last* time you had full employment.' Abraham Lincoln freed the slaves to die in the rain, to sleep on the ground because they had no house, and catch all the diseases that were available."

Speaking to five hundred newspaper editors at Washington, D.C.'s Shoreham Hotel he was critical of the way the white press handles news of black people:

"The punishment (for black spokesmen) for sounding rational and in deadly earnest is a total blackout. And I use the word advisedly.

"Today there are only two kinds of statements a black man can make and expect that the white press will report.

"First, is an attack on another black man—calling him an Uncle Tom or a fanatic or a black militant. The second is a statement that sounds radical, violent, extreme—the verbal equivalent of a riot—Watts put into words.

"Think back over the past months and ask yourselves, aren't those the only statements the press will publish? And you will begin to realize that the Negro is being rewarded by the public media only if he turns on another Negro and uses his tongue as a switchblade, or only if he sounds outlandish, extremist, or psychotic."

The speaker then invited the editors to visit ghetto areas as guests and as friends. What they would experience, he promised, is "a world you would never see except when a riot erupts and the police charge in with your reporters and photographers close at their heels." When McKissick was through the audience vigorously applauded his remarks. As editors they appreciated the soundness of his reporting.

McKissick wrote a book, *Three Fifths of a Man,* that was published by The Macmillan Company in 1969. The title came from Article 1, Section 2 of the original U. S. Constitution, an article providing that a state's representatives and taxes would be determined by the number of people making up its population. At that time all whites, only three fifths of the blacks, and no Indians at all were taken into the count.

The author points out, however, that the Thirteenth, Fourteenth, and Fifteenth Amendments give the Constitution and the Declaration of Independence the power to liberate all oppressed Americans with a minimum of hate. And McKissick proves his point by citing cases won in the nation's courts with no unpleasant aftermaths. In conclusion he recommends the establishment of cooperative business enterprises among black Americans as a vital step in the direction of their liberation.

Floyd McKissick resigned his post as CORE's National Director in the summer of 1968. His interest in developing economic strength among black Americans was beginning to occupy much of his energy and time. He established and is President of Floyd B. McKissick Enterprises, Inc., with home offices in New York's Harlem. The organization's purpose is to help organize and finance sound black businesses throughout the country. One of its prime projects is the development of Soul City, a new community in Warren County, North Carolina.

Soul City is envisioned as a community where black people can participate *fully* in its economic and social activities. At the same time it will not be a segregated city but will be open to *all* people who respect the rights and customs of others. Soul City will provide its residents with low and middle income housing, as well as normal municipal facilities. Its location will make it accessible by air, rail, and motor highway. Industry will be invited to establish plants in Soul City and along with black businesses will share profits with their workers. Soul City has received government financial aid as well as similar aid from The Chase Manhattan Bank N.A.

As he discusses his plans McKissick recalls that his father worked as head bellman at Asheville's Vanderbilt Hotel, where he served whites for the tips they gave him. One day his father called him aside and said:

"Son, there isn't going to be but one Tom in this family, and that's going to be me. So you go out and get yourself an education so you won't ever *have* to be an Uncle Tom."

It was sound advice indeed. And Ernest McKissick's son has heeded it well.

Fannie Lou Hamer

THE ASSEMBLED THRONG suddenly sat forward and upright as the plump sturdy black woman rose and walked a few feet to face the speaker. She limped slightly, the result of polio. That, however, was of scant importance to those who saw the tilt of her head and the resoluteness of her stride. It was Commencement Day 1969 at Atlanta's Morehouse College, alma mater of Martin Luther King, Jr. Among the assembled dignitaries receiving honorary degrees were Hubert H. Humphrey, the nation's former Vice-President and the Reverend Martin Luther King, Sr.

The momentary hush was broken by the speaker's voice, carried clearly over the public address system:

"Fannie Lou Hamer, you have little formal education and your speech is full of errors in grammar and diction; but you tell your story with a passionate power that is intensified by pain, and you are a natural leader with the capacity to guide and inspire your fellow sufferers. You also have the ability to awaken in your oppressed countrymen your own unquenchable yearning for freedom and equality. We pay tribute to you for your noble example of black womanhood, for your strong defense of human

dignity, and for your fearless promotion of civil rights in
your native state of Mississippi."

The applause that followed that extraordinary special
citation to Mrs. Fannie Lou Hamer must have rung a
special symphony of chimes for her. The youngest of
twenty children in a poverty-ridden Mississippi black family, she *knew* the meaning of privation and struggle. Now
at age fifty-one she could reflect with an abundance of understanding and a tiny amount of satisfaction upon the
earlier years of her life. They had not been easy and
pleasant years.

Fannie Lou Hamer, like John Stennis and James O.
Eastland, is a native of Mississippi. Unlike them she is a
woman, she is black, and she was never elected to the
United States Senate. In the ten years prior to her birth,
white Mississippians had lynched eighty-three black men,
two white men, and one black woman. The year Fannie
Lou Townsend reached her third birthday, thirteen lynchings took place in Mississippi. Only Georgia, with fourteen
lynchings, kept Mississippi out of first place.

Two years later, ten thousand of Yazoo City's black men,
women, and children fled their native Mississippi by rail,
automobile, oxcarts, and on foot. Few of them had paused
to gather up their meager belongings. Why? Because Willie
Mansfield, a young black man, had been accused (but by
no means found guilty) of attacking a white woman with
an ax, and had been burned alive by an enraged mob of
whites. And Yazoo City blacks were not sure the mob
would not suddenly turn upon them too.

Terror, *stark* terror, has long been the order of the day
—and the night—in Mississippi and other states of the deep
south. That terror as we shall later note does not exist
merely because Mississippians are "meaner" than Americans in other parts of our nation. It exists because terror

and the reasons for its use are as advantageous to some as they are *dis*advantageous to others.

Fannie Lou Hamer clearly recalls her childhood. In a 1965 interview she said:

"My parents moved to Sunflower County when I was two years old. I remember, and I never will forget, one day—I was six years old and I was playing beside the road and this plantation owner drove up to me and asked me could I pick cotton. I told him I didn't know and he said, 'Yes, you can. I will give you things that you want from the commissary store, and he named things like cracker-jacks and sardines—and it was a huge list that he called off. So I picked the thirty pounds of cotton that week, but I found out what actually happened was he was *trapping* me into beginning the work I was to keep doing; and I never did get out of his debt again."

Fannie Lou's parents tried desperately to keep their twenty children in school. That was no easy task inasmuch as they could not afford to clothe them all. Besides, school for black children was in session only four months out of the year, and the rest of the time was spent "making" the cotton crop. With fourteen boys and six girls working along with their parents it was possible for the Townsends to produce fifty-five and sixty bale crops. But they were producing for the white landowner, and little went to them. White Mississippi plantation owners rarely dealt fairly with their black workers, and their cheating usually went unchallenged. Yet Mrs. Hamer still recalls Joe Pulliam.

She remembers him as a "great Christian man" who sharecropped with a white family that cheated him out of his earnings. Some time later when the boss handed Pulliam $150 and order him to go to the hill and "buy" another black family to add to the owner's work force, Joe balked. He pocketed the $150 with the declaration that he was applying that money to what was already owed *him*.

The enraged landowner was momentarily stunned. No *black* man had ever defied *him* before. Angry words passed between them and the owner shot Joe Pulliam. Had his aim been better that would have ended the incident. Another "nigger" would have learned not to ever challenge a white man no matter what the circumstances. But Joe Pulliam, only slightly wounded, went inside his hovel and, emerging with a Winchester rifle, killed the owner on the spot. Another white man who was with the landowner at the time fled back to town to spread word of what had happened. Pulliam, knowing he was marked for a violent death, readied himself for it.

After gathering a supply of cartridges, he fled to the bayou to make his final stand in a hollow stump. Before the mob reached him with gasoline and machine gun fire Joe Pulliam had killed thirteen men and wounded twenty-six others. And as Fannie Lou recalls it, "Mississippi was a quiet place for a long time."

Meanwhile, Fannie Lou's father had managed with the help of his wife and their children to save a little in spite of the cheating that had kept them so poor. He bought mules, wagons, cultivators, and some farming equipment. And he *rented* land, because that would afford him a measure of independence. But success was not to come to the Townsends. Someone, determined that they would not "get too uppity," put Paris green in their livestock's feed trough, killing their mules and cows. "That knocked us right back down," Mrs. Hamer recalls. "And things got so tough then I began to wish I was white."

Her mother, valiantly trying to make up the loss, worked like a man. One day while using an ax she was struck in the eye by a flying splinter, an accident that eventually led to total blindness. Fannie watched her strong mother's body weaken under the strain of impoverishment. She looked at the patched clothes, the rough black hands, and she resolved then and there to seek a better life not only for her mother but for all the exploited black people of Mississippi.

A physically strong young woman herself, Fannie Townsend was twenty-four when she married Perry Hamer. America was at war with Japan and Germany and the nation's economy, bolstered by the demands of war, began a rapid climb from the depths of the depression '30s. Fannie Lou, conscious of the needs of her failing mother and a good husband, secured a job on a Mississippi plantation as a sharecropper and timekeeper. It was a job she would hold for eighteen years—until she decided in 1962 that she was going to exercise her citizen's right to vote.

To understand why voting has been, and still is, difficult and often impossible for black Mississippians, one must know something of Mississippi politics and economy and the relationship of black Mississippians to both.

Nearly a hundred years ago black people did vote freely for a time in Mississippi. In spite of their former slave status and the south's fear of what they might do in retaliation, Mississippi blacks did experience a measure of freedom under the military government set up following the Civil War. There were forty black members of the first Reconstruction Legislature of 1867. The "Black and Tan Convention" assembled in 1868 had sixteen blacks among its hundred members. The Convention drew up a constitution eliminating most voting qualifications and extending the vote to blacks and whites on the same basis. This constitution was ratified in 1869. For the first time black Mississippians were permitted by state law to vote. Indeed, they comprised a majority of the electorate.

Hiram R. Revels, first black Senator of Mississippi, served an unexpired term in Washington, Blanche K.

Bruce served there for six years, and John R. Lynch served two terms. In 1870 five black men sat in the Mississippi State Senate. The peak of black political participation in Mississippi politics was reached between 1870 and 1873.

Although black illiteracy was 80 per cent and although these black politicians were villified as illiterate pawns of northern carpetbaggers, a study of their educational backgrounds reveals that they were not the ignoramuses their enemies said they were. Hiram Revels, a North Carolinian, spent two years at a Quaker seminary in Ohio and studied at Knox College in Illinois. Blanche K. Bruce, a former Virginia slave, escaped to the north, where he studied and established a school for black students. John Lynch, with no more than a common school education, wrote and spoke with remarkable fluency.

Outnumbered Mississippi whites became alarmed. As they noted that half the voting-age blacks were registered voters, that alarm turned to panic. Would not these former slaves take over the political and the economic control of the state? And, after that, would they not repay in kind the ill treatment they had received? The hysteria created by such fears made every black man in uniform or in political office suspect.

Mississippi newspapers reflected the state's anxiety. For instance, an editorial in the July 31, 1875, issue of the *Yazoo City Banner* declared that "Mississippi is a white man's country, and by the eternal God, we'll run it." A little earlier that year the *Handsboro Democrat* for April 10, 1875, advocated "a white man's government, by white men, for the benefit of white men."

The Ku Klux Klan, which had sprung alive in 1865 in Tennessee, inspired its secret society counterpart in Mississippi, The White Line. They and similar terrorist gangs were determined to drive the black men from positions of political power and to establish undisputed white supremacy. And they had the backing of the white community.

In 1890 Mississippi with its majority black population decided that the only way to preserve White Supremacy was by completely disfranchising the blacks. But what was the best method of doing it? Some thought that to restrict voting to those who owned property would be the way. Others felt that one's intelligence and attachment to the community should be the determining measurements. But using each of these would have denied the vote to many poor whites.

Finally a method was found. Those who owned no property of a fixed value or who were the descendants of persons who had not voted before 1866 would be denied the voting right. Of course, white Mississippians could qualify if their immediate forebears had been voters. Blacks whose forebears had been slaves were automatically eliminated. Nor could many blacks qualify as landowners, as the majority were landless. It was decided also to levy an annual $2.00 poll tax on all voters and require them to read and interpret any section of the Mississippi State Constitution chosen by the examiners.

A Mississippi Convention read those requirements into law and South Carolina quickly followed. Within the next decade Louisiana, North Carolina, Alabama, Virginia, Georgia, and Oklahoma enacted similar laws restricting black voting. Moreover, black Americans were prevented by law from marrying whites, and they were banned from white schools, hotels, barber shops, restaurants, and theaters. They were compelled to ride in special sections of trains and boats since the Civil Rights Acts of 1875 had been completely overturned by the Supreme Court in 1883.

Because the severest repression of black people took place where their numbers were greatest, Mississippi became the most repressive state. Black people had to be "kept in their place" at all costs. The sharp color line even prevented two-party politics from existing, for it was feared that either party would be tempted to use black votes to punish the other.

Meanwhile, the high cost of maintaining separate (and quite unequal) facilities for the races kept the non-industrialized south materially poor. Mississippi, at one time, one of our wealthiest states, thanks to its slave population, was now the poorest of them all.

Her people were cynically exploited by shrewd politicians, who exhorted poor whites to stay alert against "the niggers." So the lynching of blacks, especially of black men, on the slightest pretext became commonplace. And as the terror continued well into the middle of the twentieth century, the political demagogues remained in power because black people were not allowed to go to the polls and vote them out of office.

Fannie Lou Hamer lived in Mississippi's Sunflower County, where in 1964 there were nearly twice as many blacks as whites of voting age. Yet the number of registered black voters there was a mere 2½ per cent of that of whites. Mrs. Hammer saw that as a shameful violation of human rights and there would be no rest for her until she did something to correct it. The memory of her mother who had just died, a blind invalid, was painfully fresh.

The Mississippi that Fannie Lou Hamer knew as a child was rapidly changing. Automation had arrived on the cotton plantations, eliminating the need for the former large number of black cotton field hands. And along with automation at least ten major industries were beginning to set up branch factories in Mississippi. Another change was in the attitude of the black working people. Many were no longer disposed to accept repression meekly. They had seen other black southerners' injustices, and they, the most severely repressed, had many reasons to express their feelings of outrage.

Now it happens that Sunflower County, where Mrs. Hamer lives, is the same Mississiippi county where Senator James Oliver Eastland owns a vast cotton plantation. And Senator Eastland, because of his Senate seniority, is one of the most powerful political leaders in Washington. He is also an ardent advocate of white supremacy, and an employer of scores of black farm workers.

During the early 1960s Senator Eastland received liberal government agricultural allotments, enabling him to plant or not to plant crops as he saw fit. There were times when the Senator and other wealthy planters chose not to keep their workers gainfully employed. But at their peak of employment, black laborers on the Eastland plantation did not earn handsome salaries.

If one doubts this he need only know how much less Sunflower County families had to live on than whites in 1960. Nearly six times as many black families as white earned less than $2000 that year. Nearly eight times as many white as black families earned more than $4000. That disparity, added to the fact of a disproportionate white vote in a county where blacks outnumber whites two-to-one, moved Mrs. Hamer to act.

It was August 1962 when two civil rights groups came to Mississippi to help black people register to vote. They were the Student Nonviolent Coordinating Committee and The Southern Christian Leadership Conference. Among those in Ruleville who heard the young Reverend James Bevel preach and James Foreman speak was Fannie Lou Hamer. The Reverened Bevel tied his text, "Discerning the Signs of the Times," to voter registration, while Foreman declared that it was the constitutional right of all those gathered to register and vote. It was agreed at the end of the meeting that eighteen of those present would turn up at the Indianola courthouse to register on the following Friday. Fannie Lou Hamer was their leader.

They rode in an old bus owned by a black man who used it during the summer for transporting local cotton field hands from one place to another. In the winter the same bus was used to transport many of the same laborers to Florida because there wasn't enough work in their rich Mississippi Delta county to provide food for their meager tables.

"What do you nigras want?" the court clerk growled at the group. Fannie Lou told him they were there to try to register to vote. The twenty-one questions sought information on the applicant's place of employment and place of residence. This was information the applicants knew very well would be turned over to the hostile White Citizens' Council. Then there was the reading and the interpreting of sections of the Mississippi State Constitution. "It was the first time," says Mrs. Hamer, "that I knew Mississippi *had* a constitution!" The test took the entire day for the eighteen to finish. White men in boots and carrying rifles sauntered in and out of the courthouse saying nothing but casting ominous glances at the black registrants.

At four-thirty the group reboarded the bus for Ruleville. A couple of miles outside Indianola they were stopped by police and ordered to get out. Then they were told to reboard the bus and return to Indianola where the driver was fined $100 for driving a bus of the *wrong color!* The court finally agreed to accept a $30 fine, which was hastily collected from the group, who were anxious to get back home.

Back in Ruleville, Mrs. Hamer found her oldest daughter and her younger cousin rushing out to meet her. The boss on whose land she had worked for eighteen years as a sharecropper and timekeeper was beside himself with rage because she had registered to vote. Her husband, Perry, confirmed the children's story before the landowner himself confronted her.

"You'll have to go back there and withdraw that thing, Fannie, or you'll have to leave," he ordered. There was no hesitancy in Fannie Lou's answer. "I didn't go down there to register for you, I went there to register for myself," she replied. That very night, the thirty-first of August, 1962, Mrs. Hamer left her home, her husband and children to stay in Ruleville with friends, the William Tuckers. Ten days later sixteen bullets were fired into the Tucker home and two local black girls who were ineligible to vote were shot by snipers.

Meanwhile, the landowner urged Perry Hamer to remain on the plantation until the end of harvest. He sollemly promised Mr. Hamer that after the harvest he could take their belongings with him when he went to join his wife. The end of harvest came, but Perry Hamer was not allowed to take his car, upon which he had been making payments for ten years. Instead, the landowner's son-in-law repossessed the car, claiming that the Hamers still owed $300 on it. Such was the tone of the sendoff as Fannie Lou began her new career as Mississippi civil rights activist from Sunflower County.

During the following year the Hamers, who had now established their own home in Ruleville, continued to be threatened by the local authorities. One night they answered a knock on their door to be confronted by an infamous local policeman. The officer was the brother of one of the men involved in the brutal murder of a fifteen-year-old Emmett Till several years earlier. After threatening the Hamers with bodily harm the man left.

A little later in the year, however, when Fannie Lou was arrested in Winona, Mississippi, in connection with

black voter registration she had a rough time of it. So
severely was she beaten that she nearly lost the sight of
her left eye. As it is, one of her kidneys has been per-
manently damaged. Still, she did not give up the work, for
as she has stated "we knew we would have to have a
change not only for the blacks in Mississippi but for the
poor whites as well."

Badly as she had been abused by officers in that Winona
jail, Fannie Lou Hamer was luckier than N.A.A.C.P. Field
Director Medgar Evers. On the very night she lay in her
dingy jail cell trying to ease the pain of her battered body,
he was murdered on his doorstep by a sniper hidden in a
nearby clump of bushes. Still, the fight had to go forward
and as soon as she was released she returned to her political
activities.

For months she tried to work with the regular Mississippi Democratic Party by first attempting to go to work
on the precinct level. She had no luck at all. Indeed, when
she attended a precinct meeting in Ruleville, her husband,
recently hired on a new job, was fired the following day.
There was only one way to attack the tight political
machine. She and her fellow workers would have to establish a political party of their own. They did, and they
named it The Mississippi Freedom Democratic Party.

The Mississippi Freedom Democratic Party was formed
well before the August 1964 Democratic Convention that
met in Atlantic City, New Jersey. Its program for getting
support among other delegates to the convention was well
organized and executed. As early as May 1964 the M.F.D.P.
opened an office in Washington, D.C., from which its
representatives worked. They traveled about the nation,
speaking at forums and conventions and informing all
who would listen of conditions in Mississippi. Those who
heard them were told that the terror characterizing life
for Mississippi black people was being perpetuated by the

very ones who had traditionally selected the regular delegates.

The M.F.D.P., by contrast, considered itself a party of the people. By its own admission the conventions in which its delegates were selected operated outside the framework of Mississippi law. Still, the M.F.D.P. did not consider itself a party of lawbreakers because from their point of view law, in the moral sense, did not and had not for years existed in Mississippi. M.F.D.P. delegates took their view from that section of the Declaration of Independence that reads:

"Whenever any form of Government becomes destructive of these ends, it is the Right of the People to alter or to abolish it, and to institute new Government."

Just what kind of people composed the Mississippi Freedom Democratic Party delegation? Who were they? Well, to begin with, they opened the convention to black and white alike. And the delegation that came out of those conventions was made up of people doing average jobs. They were tenant farmers, laborers, small landowners, a few others including clergymen, a bit more prestigious. But the majority were certainly "of the people." At the June 1964 meeting held in Jackson, Mississippi's Masonic Temple they elected white, native-born Mississippian Ed King as Chairman of its delegation. Fannie Lou Hamer was elected Vice-Chairman. For the first time in its history the old-line Mississippi politicians were being challenged before the nation and the world by their own constituents.

The M.F.D.P. did not expect things to go smoothly for them at the Democratic Convention in Atlantic City. It had to do intensive lobbying with other delegations and it had to face the Convention's Credentials Committee. So the M.F.D.P. wisely provided other delegates with copies of the brief it was submitting to the Committee on Credentials. They anticipated that committee's suspicions of them and they produced mimeographed biographies of each M.F.D.P. delegate for public inspection. Nothing was left to chance as they sought to present themselves as serious and responsible representatives of Mississippians at large.

The regular Democratic delegation, on the other hand, did not have to mount such an effort. Indeed, it had the support of President Johnson and Hubert Humphrey, who would become the next Vice-President of the United States. It had the support of organized labor, too, and of civil rights leaders who were certain Johnson and Humphrey would be elected. Humphrey meanwhile had made it clear that he was supporting the Mississippi regulars. So as the national political powerhouse revealed its strength in Atlantic City the M.F.D.P. read its own fate.

It was finally offered (and urged to settle for) a compromise. The regulars, they were informed, were going to be seated and two members of the M.F.D.P. *could* be seated as delegate-at-large at the Convention. But the choice of which two of their party would be chosen was not to be theirs. The M.F.D.P. promptly rejected the compromise and with that their hopes of replacing the Mississippi regulars withered and died.

With northern liberal help they were later able in Washington to challenge the right of the Mississippi regulars to take seats in the House of Representatives. And they forced an answer to the challenge from the Governor and other state officials who issued hasty statements condemning violence and racism in Mississippi. But the old Mississippi and national patterns of misconduct were not really being challenged. No one knew better than Fannie Lou Hamer, who later spoke of the national support given the Mississippi racists.

"You see," she said, "this is not Mississippi's problem, it is *America's* problem. All of it is America's problem.

Many, many of the threatening letters and telegrams I've received since I was on television in Atlantic City weren't from Mississippi. I've had telegrams from Chicago and other places in the north telling us what we shouldn't have done and what ought to happen to us." After a pause she added, "In Atlantic City I had a letter with a picture of a heart and a dagger through the heart, and reading under it, telling me to go back to Africa."

Well, Mrs. Hamer did make her first trip to Africa. She went in the autumn of 1964 as one of a group of eleven Americans invited by the government of Guinea. She recalls how pleasantly they were received there and that they were called upon by President Sékou Touré. With her typical and practical candor she notes the irony of having to go thousands of miles to a so-called land of "savage heathens" to be personally greeted and made welcome by the head of a foreign nation.

Fannie Lou Hamer is kept quite busy as a lecturer, traveling from her modest Ruleville, Mississippi, home to various parts of the nation. Because she sees Mississippi's problems and, indeed, the problems of humanity at large in similar and uncomplicated terms her remarks are pungently quotable. Here are a few samples.

On the nation's Liberals:

"I want to talk about some things I've seen all over the country and not just in Mississippi. We know what they think of us down here. But if all the liberals were concerned about what happens in Mississippi five congressmen wouldn't have been seated last January."

On vigilance in the national capital:

"When we went to Washington to contest the seating of the Mississippi five, the way we were treated, you would have thought we were at the jailhouse in Indianola (Miss.) . They were so busy watching and keeping us out a Nazi sneaked onto the floor of the House. Things are happening in this country right under our noses."

On Vietnam and Mississippi:

"I sent a telegram to L.B.J. and told him to please bring home those troops out of Vietnam where they have no business anyhow, and bring them to Mississippi and Louisiana, because if this is a Great Society, I'd hate to see a bad one."

On the relationship between the word and the deed:

"I've been to the Agriculture Department to speak. My people said afterwards, 'Oh, Mrs. Hamer, you really told it to them.' But I go home and we're still hungry."

Fannie Lou Hamer has done more than talk. She is the author of a practical plan for feeding Sunflower County's poor blacks, and feeding them with dignity. Freedom Farms, which she conceived, gets right to the vitals of the County's problems. As Mrs. Hamer says:

"You can give a man some food and he'll eat it. Then he'll be hungry again. But give a man some ground and he'll never be hungry no more."

A black man sold the group some land. And Freedom Farms—already in possession of fifty-nine acres of black Mississippi Delta earth—provides plots of ground to its occupants. They pick their cotton by hand, can their butter beans, and eat their greens. They raise their hogs, too, from their "pig bank," and a heifer bank is envisioned to add beef to the protein diet.

More land is needed for the housing of Freedom Farms' growing inhabitants, and hopes for getting it and the minimum half acre for each home are high. Moreover, the aim is individual ownership of land and house through F.H.A. mortgage help. Mrs. Hamer wants no child on Freedom Farms to experience the uncertainty of the tenant farm living she knows only too well.

The esteem in which Fannie Lou Hamer is held by black people is important to her. She knows how frequently the title of "leader" has been conferred upon blacks by whites who can't seem to differentiate between a true leader and someone black who happens personally to appeal to them. Knowing this well and knowing hard times equally well steels Mrs. Hamer against the numbing influence of glib drawing-room flattery. The honor that was hers at that 1969 Morehouse College Commencement ceremony was not of that cut. And she received that honor with the earthy and dignified simplicity befitting a woman of valor—and greatness.

Charles Evers

THE TWO MEN and the woman walked abreast. The slender man with the narrow shoulders walked in the middle holding the hand of the woman on his left. His other wrist was handcuffed to that of the heavier man wearing a badge and a holstered revolver. It was an incredible scene in this small, humid Mississippi town called Fayette, for the prisoner and his wife were white and the arresting officer black.

Forty-eight-year-old Dale Walton, a former Grand Dragon of the Ku Klux Klan, had been stopped as he drove into Fayette, a rebel flag fluttering from his radio antenna. An anonymous white caller had telephoned a warning that Fayette's Mayor would be assassinated and Walton was carrying a small arsenal of loaded guns in his car. The newly elected black Mayor, Charles Evers, had escaped a direct attempt on his life, an attempt similar to one that five years earlier had been fatal to his younger brother, Medgar.

That Evers was the Mayor of Fayette and the arresting officer was his Chief of Police were due to a number of new and revolutionary circumstances in Mississippi. Not the least of them was Evers' own previous work in getting the black majority of Fayette out to vote for him. Another was that his martyred brother, Medgar, had worked through the N.A.A.C.P. to secure voting rights for blacks. Still a third was the valiant work, already described, of Fannie Lou Hamer and the Mississippi Freedom Democratic Party.

Life began for Charles Evers on September 11, 1922, in the quiet country town of Decatur in east-central Mississippi. There were few black residents in Decatur then and while most of them were quite poor the Evers family fared relatively well. James Evers, operating an undertaking establishment and a lumber contracting firm, was a successful business man in the black community. He and his wife, Jessie, were able to provide a comfortable home for their two sons, Charles and Medgar. Charley was two years his brother's senior; the two were always very close. As children they played together and they went to school together.

They could not have been more than eleven and nine years old when one day they sauntered into a crowd gathered around the steps of Decatur's Newton County courthouse. Old Senator Theodore ("The Man") Bilbo was back home from Washington on vacation and he was delivering another of his demagogic tirades in support of white supremacy in Mississippi. Catching sight of the Evers brothers he shouted to the crowd:

"You see them two little niggers settin' down there? If you don't stop 'em one of 'em will be up here on these steps one day trying to go to Congress!"

Charley and Medgar Evers never forgot that comment Bilbo directed at them. Indeed, it planted an idea in their minds that neither was ever to abandon.

The idea grew stronger and stronger each day the Evers brothers walked the two miles to the Decatur Consolidated School for black children. As they trudged the road a familiar shiny yellow bus full of white children whizzed by. And whenever the road was muddy and sloppy the Evers children and their black companions had to scamper out of the way to avoid being splashed by the churning wheels. The humiliation of it became deeply etched in their young minds.

Charley and Medgar were barely in their teens when a neighbor, who was one of their father's friends, was seized by a white mob and dragged through the streets to the nearby fairgrounds. What had the man done that would cause a mob to enter and forcibly drag him away from his home? Someone later said he had "insulted a white woman." James and Jessie Evers hustled their boys in off the street as the mob howled and raced by with its victim.

But the boys learned the terrible details later. Because their father was the local undertaker for black folks they discovered that their neighbor's body had been so brutally mutilated that embalming was impossible. So Charley and Medgar Evers, while shielded from the terrors of hunger, were fully exposed along with other Mississippi blacks to the terrors of racism.

The two brothers were as different in temperament as in appearance. Medgar, the younger, never as large as Charley, was mild-mannered and soft-spoken. His was the scholarly, diplomatic, and suave personality. And there was a genuine humility in Medgar. Charley, taller and heavier, was, from the very beginning, brash, brusque, and outspoken. If he happened to tread heavily upon someone as he went about his daily life, so be it. For him life was simply a big rough-and-tumble scramble for existence and he was prepared to scramble with the best of them.

Charley went to high school in nearby Newton, where he lived in the home of a white restaurant owner for whom he worked after school hours. Mrs. Payne was a kindly woman who, within the framework of local custom, treated black employees well. Charley soon noted the two restaurant entrances, one for whites, the other for blacks. Resenting it, he took advantage of his employee's status by entering through the section marked for whites. No one ever challenged him, though he did once ask Mrs. Payne why the side for blacks was so *dirty*. Her answer to him was that since the dirt bothered him he would have to keep it clean.

Charley finished the eleventh grade before volunteering for military service in the Pacific just after the Japanese attacked Pearl Harbor. For five years he served in a segregated unit that did all the dirty chores. So when he returned home in 1946 he followed his father's advice and set out to earn a college degree.

First, however, he and Medgar decided that as war veterans of voting age they would have to make an effort to vote. At first they were denied the right to register. But they soon overcame that by convincing the reluctant registrar that the poll tax did not apply to veterans returning from World War II. Between registration and voting, however, word circulated around town that "those uppity Evers niggers" were "stirring up trouble." And Senator Bilbo was back on the Decatur courthouse steps declaring that "the best way to keep a nigger away from the polls on election day is to visit him the night before."

A threatening telephone call to their parents' home failed to stop the two brothers, who rose early and drove to Decatur, arriving by the time the polls opened. Not another black man or woman was in sight as Charles and Medgar with four friends entered the courthouse. Outnumbered by armed white men carrying rifles, they explained quietly that they were there for one purpose only: to vote. Tension grew tight as they found the door leading to the ballot box blocked by white men. All of the whites were people the Evers brothers knew. Some had been childhood playmates.

A white woman suddenly broke the tension by dramatically and tearfully advising Charles to defer. "It's not worth it, Charles—not now. You'll get a chance later," she pleaded. The six black men turned and walked out of the courthouse. Back in the fresh morning sunlight their dry throats and lungs sucked in the welcome air. True, they hadn't voted just then. But they'd be back. Releasing their grip on the loaded pistols deep in their pockets, they climbed into their car and headed home.

Alcorn A. & M. College in Lorman, Mississippi, takes pride in the fact that Hiram Revels had been its first black President. Revels had also been a U. S. Senator from Mississippi during the Reconstruction. Both Charley and Medgar enrolled at Alcorn and both, in addition to being good students, played football. Medgar, quick and shifty, played halfback. Charley, a shade under six feet and weighing only 180 pounds, held the tough and scrappy center position for four straight years.

Dr. J. R. Otis, Alcorn's President at that time, has described Charley Evers as a young man with an eye to business.

"He was always hustling around looking for a way to make a dollar during his student days. The Evers brothers are serious and dependable no-nonsense fellows. They've been a great influence here at Alcorn."

Before and even after graduation in 1950 Charley Evers kept himself busy on the campus, at home in Decatur, and in nearby Philadelphia, Mississippi, where he carried on various enterprising activities.

Following another year of military service in Korea with his reserve unit, Charley settled in Philadelphia, Mississippi, not to teach as he had trained to do but to pursue the life of an entrepreneur. There he established a hotel, a taxi business, and a gas station; and he began to earn a handsome living. But Charley Evers wasn't satisfied.

Even then, he had an eye on the possibilities of a career in politics, for he began to push for a greater registration of black voters in and around Philadelphia, Mississippi.

Medgar, a business administration major, was working meanwhile for the Magnolia Mutual Life Insurance Company in the all-black Mississippi town of Mound Bayou. He also began to organize boycotts against gas station operators who refused to let black patrons use their rest rooms. And he sought to establish N.A.A.C.P. chapters in as many areas as he could reach. Charley began to work similarly with the N.A.A.C.P. in Philadelphia. But Neshoba County was a particularly festering center of Ku Klux Klan activity and any meetings designed to unite blacks against white tyranny had to be held in strict secrecy.

Barns and open pastures were used by Charley Evers and his followers for small group meetings until pressures against them began to rise to a dangerous level. It was, it developed, impossible to keep their civil rights activities secret. And even though membership cards from the N.A.A.C.P. offices in New York were mailed in unmarked envelopes, news of their activities leaked to hostile whites. The men who worked in Charley's establishments were threatened by Klansmen. Credit became almost impossible for him to obtain.

Charley Evers had become Mississippi's pioneer black disk jockey and, as could be expected, racist callers would threaten him and the station from which he broadcast. Finally in sheer disgust he decided the success he was having simply wasn't worth the harassment. He would have to leave Mississippi. Before he left, however, his brother, now Field Director of the N.A.A.C.P. office in Jackson, reminded Charley of a pact they had made on that tense day in Decatur when they had first tried to vote. The brothers had agreed that if any disaster should befall one of them as he engaged in civil rights activity the other would carry on the work left by the first. Now reaffirming that resolution, the two sealed it with a solemn handshake and Charley headed his new Ford onto Route 61 with Chicago as his destination.

Chicago 1957 neither halted nor diminished the ambitions of the husky young man from Philadelphia, Mississippi. With his uncanny grasp of human nature and a driving urge to "get ahead" he took a job hauling sides of beef in the Swift Packing House during the day. At night he worked as washroom attendant in fancy hotels in the famed Loop area and on weekends he tended bar at a tavern. With eyes and ears receptive to all that came within their range, Charley Evers was rapidly becoming acquanited, firsthand, with big city ways.

In a very short time he had enough money to open a cocktail lounge of his own, and this was shortly followed by the opening of a second lounge. Five years later, with his talent for driving bargains along with a measure of good fortune, Evers had become prosperous. As a businessman he combined shrewdness with sheer nerve. At one point he risked the ire of the Chicago syndicate by refusing to use their juke boxes in his cocktail lounges. He bought his own. It was June 1963 when Medgar heard of his brother's outright defiance of the vaunted power of the Chicago mobsters. Medgar was worried and he telephoned Charley.

"Charley *please* be more careful. You'll find those fellows up there just as ruthless as these crackers down here," he implored. If Charley shared his brother's concern it wasn't evident in his response. "Don't worry about it, little brother. I'll handle these cats up here. You just keep your eyes on those rednecks down there." Tough, hard-voiced Charley was as brash and self-assured as ever. Within a few days a sniper's fatal bullet had found its way in Medgar's back, and Charles, recalling their pact, quickly cleared his business in Chicago and returned to Mississippi to carry on Medgar's work.

If officials in the N.A.A.C.P.'s national office were shocked by the grim swiftness with which their Jackson representative had been murdered, they were equally shocked by the swiftness of his brother's takeover. Forty-eight hours before Medgar's remains were buried in Arlington National Cemetery, Charles was in command at the Jackson office. When asked about it later he replied bluntly and directly, "I wasn't going to let anybody mess up what he had done. I knew nobody else could do (the job) like I could." Official N.A.A.C.P. comment was that Mr. Evers' appointment was temporary and that a permanent Field Director would be named later. However, with his wife, Nannie, and three small daughters following close behind him, Charles Evers was re-establishing himself on old and familiar ground.

N.A.A.C.P. officers who had enjoyed a warm relationship with Medgar watched anxiously as Charles, with considerably less elegance of style, plunged into his new work. His speech then was halting, but his thinking was quick, sound, and practical. Using the N.A.A.C.P. as a base, he began to build his organization in southwestern Mississippi, where there had been practically no civil rights activity. Natchez was a prime target.

Knowing how the rural southern black community gravitated to its churches, Charles first sought the support of the clergy. When he explained that his program would unify their flocks and thereby *strengthen them as leaders,* the ministers listened. Then moving on into the communities he talked with the hard-working masses and the unemployed. He told them of the value of complaining about their poor conditions—not mere individual grumbling, but *organized mass* complaining where the authorities could *hear* it. Then with the ministers anxious to strengthen their positions, and their followers anxious to strengthen theirs, Evers was ready to fire his big gun—the economic boycott. He had convinced the black citizens of Natchez of the wisdom of staying out of the white man's stores until some of their demands were met.

The Natchez merchants were, of course, furious. They threatened and fumed but eventually they made concessions. For the first time in its citizens' memory black workers were hired in Natchez as policemen, clerks, and salesmen. A hospital that had been tightly segregated let down its color bar. With this success the Evers' forces moved in on Port Gibson and Fayette. Meanwhile, a white backlash incident in Natchez, blood-chilling though it was, did not halt the program. An N.A.A.C.P. member, Wharlest Jackson, was killed by a bomb placed under the seat of the truck he was driving. Within hours Charles Evers was on the scene organizing a massive protest march as worried city officials wondered aloud to Evers how best to cope with their city's unrest. Evers, visibly angry, promised nothing other than that his people would retaliate in kind if attacked by whites, as the latter swore they intended to do. After Evers made his pronouncement there was no such attack. Instead, Evers got the Mayor *to agree to appear at a civil rights rally,* an *unheard*-of maneuver in Mississippi. Moreover, before the evening was over Mayor John Nosser of Natchez, Mississippi, had linked arms with blacks and joined them in singing "We Shall Overcome."

Meanwhile, the Evers strategy was spreading into Wilkinson, Franklin, Claiborne, and Copiah counties and a strong following for Charles Evers was in the making. Along with his local work Evers had developed a profound sense of the importance of preserving unity among the nation's black leaders *outside* Mississippi. Many of the latter, especially the young, were displeased as Evers openly criticized their particular brand of black power exhortations. Along with getting phenomenal results without consulting them, he had quietly but firmly answered their criticism of his methods in the following way, "If you think you can get guns and outshoot all these murdering whites you're wrong."

Had the younger people really thought about what Evers told them, they would have realized he was not talking out of pure emotion. Several times previously he had personally risked death. Only a few months before he had stood at the base of the Jefferson County Confederate Memorial and defied fifty armed white men. To the cheers of black listeners he had shouted to the whites, "If you don't bring trouble you won't get it. But if you bring it you're going to get it." Not a white man moved to use his gun, and Evers got away with his threat. But he was no fool and he knew how to calculate the odds.

His young black critics, however, were stung by his scolding and in their anger were resolved to get even with Charles Evers. So when James Meredith, who had been wounded on his solitary march through Mississippi, returned with others to complete that march the young dissidents saw their chance for revenge. In Jackson where the march ended, spokesmen for CORE and SNCC did not invite Evers to the platform. Nor did any speaker make mention of the Evers brothers during the ensuing ceremony. One of the ironies of this was that the very platform from which Evers had been barred was one for which he had personally paid. It was a small snub and tough Charley Evers was big enough to ignore it. Moreover, he would soon go his antagonists one better by showing them the definition of unity.

During the following spring James Meredith, then living in New York City, had been approached by political foes of Adam Clayton Powell. Would Meredith, who had risked death to integrate the University of Mississippi, be willing to run against the flamboyant Harlem Congressman in a special Congressional election? Meredith agreed and elements of the nation's press were ecstatic. The arrogant and controversial Powell had at last met young *black* opposition in a man who had been in international headlines.

Black leaders all over the country were alarmed and they leveled harsh criticism at James Meredith. While they were fuming, Charley Evers slipped quietly into New York from Jackson, and went directly to see the Merediths at their apartment. Within three hours of the unannounced visit Meredith told the press he was withdrawing from the contest. Evers in a later interview with black newsman Ted Poston minimized his achievement:

"Hell, there wasn't that much to it. Everybody was talking *about* the boy and nobody had gone to talk *to* him. After all, we're both Mississippi boys with all that means. So don't credit me. He made up his own mind after thinking the situation over."

Back in Mississippi, Evers was preparing to merge his civil rights activities with politics. As he had so often told his rural listeners, the only way to get rid of a corrupt public official is by registering and then by voting him out of office. It is the Evers technique to have not just one but a *number* of black candidates selected to run for office. He knows that black candidates have varying degrees of voter appeal just as white candidates do. A coordinator is then appointed for each district and the coordinator selects workers who get the voters out to the polls. Names of all who vote are checked off and twice each day (at noon and at 4 P.M.) each district compiles its list of those who have failed to vote. Workers are quickly dispatched to seek out the nonvoter to coax them to the polls before closing time. That is how Charley Evers gets out the vote on election day.

But even before that it is not only his talking to voters but his manner of talking and the active follow-through that gets results. He has been known to scold and to threaten when he deemed it necessary. "You all voted for the white man," he bluntly accused one audience. Brushing aside their feeble protests, he proceeded to tell them he had studied the returns and that the same error couldn't be committed again:

"*You* are the ones who keep denying yourselves decent homes, decent jobs, decent schools. It ain't *never* gonna change until you send some of our own people down there to represent us at the courthouse."

Evers was even more pointed upon another occasion as he instructed his taxi drivers:

"I don't want you to haul a single Negro who gets in your car and starts talking about how he ain't gonna vote for no niggers. Just put him out right then and there."

His methods come in for criticism, especially from outsiders who get a look at his team of black "defenders." This is a unit of about sixty youths who stand ready to ward off attacks by the Ku Klux Klan and other hostile white groups. That the youths are frequently referred to as the "goon squad" doesn't faze realist Evers, who has never forgotten the armed white men sauntering in and out of the Newton courthouse the morning he and Medgar tried to vote. Indeed, as is true of southern men, black and white alike, he protects his home and family with a loaded weapon, and rarely is he away from home without arms and a bodyguard.

Evers has been blamed for the alleged "jostling" of black shoppers emerging from boycotted stores with purchases. His accusers have charged him with deliberately using strong-arm methods to assure the success of the boycott and he has consistently denied the charges. It has been harder to prove that Evers, himself, ordered the "jostlings" than that they have occurred. Still, the fact that the boycotts worked to the economic advantage of the Mississippi black communities where they took place, overshadowed for most blacks the details of how they were carried out. Most of all, they brought black voters together in a way they had never before been solidified. With that accomplished, Evers was ready to make his bid for political strength.

Late in January 1968 he made an announcement that startled Mississippi and the nation. He was taking leave of his post as Field Director for the N.A.A.C.P. to run for the Congressional seat vacated by John Bell Williams, who had been elected Governor of Mississippi. For twenty-one years Williams had represented that twelve-county, Third Congressional District in southwest Mississippi, the precise area in which Evers had been doing his "revolutionary" work.

Evers would be running against six white segregationist opponents and he reasoned that he would have to close ranks with any and all other local black political groups. His first move in this direction was to make Laurence Guyot his campaign manager. Guyot was state Chairman of the Mississippi Freedom Democratic Party (M.F.D.P.) of which Fannie Lou Hamer was a leader.

Evers conducted a strong nonracist campaign, stressing improvements in welfare, expanded medicare program, and Federal aid to schools. He topped the six white candidates, pulling well ahead of his closest rival with a lead of four thousand votes. But he knew that in the required runoff vote he would be defeated, since those whites who voted for the other candidates would throw their support to his rival. That is exactly what happened as forty-one-year-old Charles H. Griffin, administrative aide to Governor Williams, defeated Evers with a voting margin of two to one. At the Griffin victory headquarters, Evers surprised everyone with an unannounced appearance where he warmly congratulated the winner. And white Mississippians applauded the gesture.

That he had been able to poll forty thousand predominantly black votes in southwest Mississippi was no small victory in Charles Evers' view. The total vote was scarcely more than two hundred thousand, and more than half of that was white. In spite of the fact that during the campaign he was subjected to harassment, including a subpoena to answer a speeding charge, and a shotgun blast at his home, Charles Evers was hopeful. He'd try again at another time and in another place.

The time was 1969, the place Fayette (Jefferson County), Mississippi. Fayette's population is approximately 1700. Evers chose Fayette simply because there was no other place in Mississippi, except the all-black communities, where the population majority is black. He had no illusions that he would win, say, in Jackson, Vicksburg, or Meridian. Jefferson County was listed in the 1960 census as having the lowest per capita ($494) income in the state. One third of its population was functionally illiterate. Its ratio of three blacks to one white was the highest in the nation. Young people seeking work were leaving Jefferson County in alarming numbers because mechanical cotton pickers had left them no work to do there.

When Evers ran for Mayor he won easily, polling 98 per cent of Fayette's black vote. His job has been one of rebuilding a decaying town and of trying to keep it an integrated one. Thus far only a few of Fayette's whites have left. Those who remain did not necessarily vote for Evers nor do they relish his being their Mayor. Still, they know that whatever he does for Fayette will benefit them.

They resentfully recall the boycott that completely crushed some white businesses and crippled others. Some have gone so far as to say that Evers used the boycotts against them to boost his own business establishments. Even those blacks who won't echo the charge chortle that the Evers enterprises did not suffer during the boycott. "I don't have to boycott whites to get business," Evers retorts. The steady flow of customers in and out of his shopping center when there is no boycott proves his point. In their resentment they forgot that they had fired one of the town's present black aldermen from the meager job he previously held. His offense had been to participate in the boycott which the whites were sure would fail.

Even more than the boycott the majority of Fayette's whites resent Evers' own newly built shopping center named after his slain brother. Though rarely patronized by whites, his combination lounge, ballroom, grocery store, liquor store, radio repair shop, laundromat, and dry cleaning plant does a brisk business among blacks. "So who's boycotting who?" Evers snaps. There was the small memorial slab, a tribute to Medgar, that Mayor Evers had erected in Fayette's park.

There the county had also set up its own memorial to its Confederate dead. Local whites resented the Evers slab, with its inscription, a quotation attributed to Kenya's Jomo Kenyatta:

" 'One of the greatest affronts to human dignity, which I have always opposed, is that of racialism.'—sayeth Kenyatta."

After two months of arguing with the white Board of County Supervisors, Evers ordered the slab removed from the park. He had it placed in the equally prominent front lawn of City Hall.

Evers does have a modicum of white verbal support in Fayette. Albert Lehmann, an automobile dealer and a local "moderate," has said he welcomes Evers or anybody else who can halt the downhill slide the town has slipped into over the past half century. The editor of the segregationist *Fayette Chronicle,* Mrs. Marie Walker, has declared of Evers, "If anybody can do anything about it (the town's decline) he's the one." A man who declared he personally didn't ever want to get too close to niggers, did remark that any future Fayette had depended upon "the niggers and those who can get close to them—those who want to."

Comments of black Fayette citizens are generally more favorable, though not always wholly endorsing. There are those who, having not personally benefited from the election of Evers, are envious of those who have. Others are envious of their Mayor, who obviously is a man of affluence. They look at his business establishments and his car and they are critical of his maintaining a home in Jackson and one in Fayette. Evers says dryly:

"White folks have three and four homes. Why can't I have just two? I get $75 a month for being Mayor of this town and I turn it over to little old ladies who need it. Sure, I like to make money and you'd better believe it. But I've worked hard for what I have. Why should it bother anybody?"

Black citizens who run afoul of the law and expect to be dealt with more leniently than whites are shocked that they can't get away with it. At one point the black Police Chief and his three full-time officers, one of them white, resigned, complaining that Public Safety Director Alfonso Deal was "too hard." Deal, a black lawman, went to work for one year in Fayette on a $10,000 grant. He is a fifteen-year veteran of the Philadelphia, Pennsylvania, police department.

Then there were the black policeman and the white city attorney who left Fayette to be married. They say Evers fired them and he says they terminated themselves. Meanwhile, the Mayor reminds his critics that Mississippi has not grown so liberal as to welcome to its bosom a black man and his mini-skirted white bride.

"Why man," he exclaimed to U.P.I. editor H. D. Quigg, "this would have to be an armed camp here. We would have had to have every policeman we could find to guard and protect it."

Evers is keenly conscious of eyes, many not friendly, riveted upon every move made in Fayette under a black Mayor. "Blacks," says Evers, "haven't yet learned to take orders from blacks. And we have to get over that hurdle." He does now have four full-time and two part-time policemen. And there are those founding members of the "new" Fayette who remain fiercely loyal to the new approach. The five black aldermen who were elected along with Evers exude nothing less than confidence in their ability to do their job well.

Howard Chambliss, who works at the dry cleaning shop in the Medgar Evers Shopping Center, admits his deficiencies in reading and spelling. But he is sure of the soundness of his judgment and the soundness of his decision to go along with the Evers program. Isaiah Anderson, a lumber yard worker, is organizing a local of the United Mine Workers. James Gale is a tough truck driver. He was one of the first two black men to vote in Jefferson County and he was an N.A.A.C.P. organizer. Gale makes it clear to all that he will settle for nothing less than first-class citizenship.

Thirty-nine-year-old Will Turner, who is the youngest of the aldermen, has his own construction business, thanks to an FHA loan and the knowledge that black men could apply for one. The oldest of the aldermen is sixty-six-year-old Ferdinand Allen, an itinerant and successful vegetable dealer with an uncanny business sense, who describes his life's experience as having taken him "up the rough side of the mountain."

Evers has white assistants who have come in from northern cities and one of Fayette's former white employees has remained to continue work as Fire Chief. He is Carl Weiner, a shoemaker by trade, whose wife urged him to quit his post as Fire Chief. But Weiner refused to go, even as he had earlier refused to join the Ku Klux Klan. He simply could not see the good sense of alienating black friends who would most likely also be customers, just to satisfy the racist dictates of the Klan. Evers, of course, encourages any white person, with skills and the will to help, to join forces with him and his fellow citizens.

Plans for Fayette include the encouragement of big industry to locate a plant or two there. Jobs are the community's number one need. Once they are available a great deal more will have to be done before the town can hope to free itself from the morass that years of neglect have imposed upon it. A sewage system must be installed and so must paved streets and sidewalks. Housing is Fayette's number two need, as the shanties in the east side of town attest. Fayette residents have never had the advantage of ambulance service, and only recently has a new water line been installed in the section occupied by its poorest inhabitants. These are the major needs. There are dozens of minor ones.

If the impression here is that Mr. Evers faces a prodigious job as Mayor of tiny Fayette, Mississippi, that impression is totally accurate. As much as any of us, he loves life. Yet if he must give up life in this struggle, he has made it plain that he will be fighting all the way as he does. Charles Evers is just that kind of man.

Carl B. Stokes

THE WHITE-DOMINATED SCHOOL BOARD had spoken with swift finality as it curtly declined to grant the polite request. The inauguration of Charles Evers would most certainly *not* take place in a Fayette, Mississippi, school. Nor would former Mayor Allen dare agree to swear in his black successor. So the Mayor-elect and his well-wishers gathered in a local parking lot, where, under the broiling July sun, the formal ceremony took place. Metropolitan Opera star Leontyne Price, a native Mississippian, had flown in from New York to sing the National Anthem. She was not the only visiting black celebrity, for others included Whitney Young, Jr., Julian Bond, and Carl B. Stokes. Only two years before, Mr. Stokes had, himself, been inaugurated as the first black Mayor of Cleveland, Ohio.

Although Cleveland's population of eight hundred thousand would seem to make any comparison with tiny Fayette, Mississippi, completely ludicrous, the two black Mayors share several common mayoral experiences. Evers was the first black man to be elected Mayor of a deep south town of black and white citizens. Stokes was the first black to become a Mayor of a major American city.

When Evers became its chief executive, Fayette was a dying southern town. Cleveland, when Stokes took office in November 1967, was a colorless industrial city that could move in only one direction—up. Its previous administration, like that of Fayette, had done little to improve the expanding city. In thirty-eight years only four multistoried buildings had been erected there. Worried whites were fleeing the inner city for the suburbs, taking badly needed tax dollars with them. While Fayette needs water lines installed throughout its black section, Cleveland's Cuyahoga River is so industrially polluted as to constitute a fire hazard.

Just as Fayette's two populations, black and white, are kept separate by local law, so are Cleveland's black East Side and white West Side kept separate by custom. Charles Evers and Carl Stokes are Democrats who received the enthusiastic support of their respective black constituents. Evers' black constituency composed the majority of Fayette's population. Stokes' black supporters were 38 per cent of Cleveland's voters. A sprinkling of whites, sure that Fayette could not fare as badly under a black Mayor, as it already had lent support to Evers. The same was true in Cleveland as a minority of whites, truly concerned with their city's future, lent their support to Stokes.

Both candidates, running in traditionally Democratic communities, managed to win without heavy party support. The Stokes victory prompted Floyd McKissick, then National Director of CORE, to remark:

"A black man is still a black man and the parties do not support black candidates with the same vim, vigor, and vitality that they do white candidates."

Handsome Carl Burton Stokes has never forgotten he is black.

He was born in Cleveland's central ghetto area in 1927. When little Carl was barely two years old, his father, Charles Stokes, an unskilled laundry worker, died suddenly. Widowed Louise Stokes, with two small boys to support, went to work as a domestic. But the times were hard. The stock market had crashed, plunging the nation into an economic depression and work, even for black domestics, was scarce. Louise Stokes was forced to apply for welfare assistance, working as a maid in the homes of any whites who would hire her.

For ten years she, and her sons, Louis and Carl, shared one bedroom with the rats and the cockroaches so indigenous to slum cities. Whenever Louise Stokes was able to get steady domestic work, she left both boys with their grandmother to keep them off the streets and out of trouble. Louis and Carl were constantly admonished by both mother and grandmother to "study so you'll become somebody."

Both boys helped their mother by selling newspapers and doing odd jobs in neighborhood stores. Like slum neighborhoods everywhere, theirs was tough. Fighting was a normal part of daily existence. A boy developed into either a first-rate street-fighter or a first-rate track man, and if he was particularly adaptable, he became both. Carl and his companions quite normally worshipped the image of Joe Louis, the famed "Brown Bomber" who was the current world's heavyweight boxing champion. So deep indeed is the slum boy's respect for fighting skill that Carl, who liked also to read, found it necessary to hide his borrowed books under his coat on trips to and from the library. Had his pool-hall pals seen him carrying books, Carl would have to fight just to prove he wasn't "going soft." Reading books is not considered the "in thing" among tough slum kids.

Although a good student, Carl, sensitive to his family's material poverty, left high school in order to earn some money. But there was little for him, a dropout, to do except take a job at hard labor in a steel foundry. As soon as he turned eighteen he joined the Army and served with the U.S. forces in Germany before deciding he ought to complete his schooling. Returning to Cleveland, he re-entered high school from which he was graduated in 1947. During the next eighteen months he was a psychology major at West Virginia State College, and during the following two years at Western Reserve University.

In the interim, he had taken a job as chauffeur for an organizer in the gubernatorial campaign of Frank Lausche. After the Lausche victory Carl was offered a state job and he chose to be a liquor inspector. It was a tough job. His very first case took him to an unlicensed saloon where the rough barkeep and his customers laughed in the slender young inspector's face and advised him to "get lost." Carl's ghetto upbringing and Army experience responded automatically. He promptly pistol-whipped the arrogant barkeep into submission as the customers fled for cover.

Upon a later occasion he emerged the solitary victor in a shoot-out with a group of bootleggers, and upon resigning from the service in 1950 his record for making arrests was the highest among eighty-five inspectors. He also had earned a college degree and had decided upon a career in law. At the University of Minnesota Carl took his B.S. in law, working meanwhile as a dining car waiter. He then earned his LL.B. degree by attending night classes at the Cleveland-Marshall Law School while working days as a court probation officer. Again young Stokes was well qualified by experience for his job. Many of the delinquent youngsters with whom he worked in the courts came from the same neighborhood in which he grew up and from which he has not fled.

On the very day in 1957 Carl Stokes passed the Ohio bar examination he gave up his court job and entered the practice of law with his older brother, Louis. He had meanwhile met and married attractive Shirley Edwards, a library science major and a graduate of Fisk University.

Carl B. Stokes

It was 1958 and Cleveland's Mayor Anthony Celebreeze appointed him assistant prosecutor under City Law Director Ralph Locker. Prosecutor Stokes barely thirty-one years old was rising quickly.

For four years he worked in that office and in 1962 was elected at age thirty-five to the Ohio Legislature. He was the first black Democrat to so serve his state and at the end of his three terms in office was hailed by a fellow representative as "one of the most effective and hardest working members in the House of Representatives." Among his achievements were his work in gaining tough air-pollution controls—a much needed item in any industrialized city. Stokes also helped draft legislation establishing a state department of urban affairs. He wrote a new mental health services act, promoted a gun-control bill, and helped strengthen the city's traffic regulations. He was the only Democrat to sponsor a bill giving the Governor the power to dispatch the National Guard into a city before a riot could get out of control.

Then there was still another Stokes achievement in the State Legislature that incidentally was beneficial to his brother. Carl had led the fight for Congressional redistricting but the move was not successful. Undismayed he formed a group of lawyers to get the issue into the courts. It was his brother, Louis, who helped to argue successfully the case before the U.S. Supreme Court. (Cleveland was indeed redistricted for elections that were to take place six years later in 1968 and Louis Stokes ran and won a Congressional seat for himself.)

Ever the conscientious student, Carl Stokes began to pore through the records of the most recent Cleveland municipal elections. He studied them precinct by precinct. Then on a cold night in 1963 he gathered five close friends around him in his basement apartment. Citing what he had discovered in his research he told them that Cleveland's black voters definitely had the strength to over-throw the worn-out political machine of Cleveland. "One of us," he exclaimed, "could be Mayor of this city!" None of those sitting with him wondered which one Carl Stokes was thinking about.

When in 1964 Carl seriously entertained notions of becoming Cleveland's chief executive, the city was far from being at its best. Its 168-year-old proud history had begun to lose its venerable meaning as industries failed to supply enough work to employ its ghetto dwellers. And Cleveland had ghettos. With a huge group of white blue-collar workers of European origin and a steadily increasing black population of southern labor recruits vying with each other for jobs, the city was becoming polarized. And as both city and state governments failed to find solutions to ghetto needs, ghetto inhabitants grew increasingly bitter. Cleveland's poor cynically substituted the city's slogan, "Best Location in the Nation," with one of their own, "The Mistake on the Lake." The year 1964 had become for Cleveland one of crisis.

The first indication of trouble came with a confrontation between a coalition of black and white clergymen and the Board of Education. The former demanded integrated schooling and the latter replied by building more schools in the black ghetto. A tragic climax occured when the Reverend Bruce W. Klunder, a white clergyman, was crushed to death by a bulldozer as he engaged in a civil rights protest.

The smoldering effects of the shocking death on Cleveland's black population were rekindled when Cleveland's Police Chief, Richard R. Wagner, demanded that Ohio retain the death penalty. The main reason why Chief Wagner made the recommendation was that a black organization, the Revolutionary Action Movement (RAM) was allegedly moving into Cleveland. RAM's objective, declared Chief Wagner, was to "overthrow the Government of the United States and incidentally shoot all the Caucasians." Abolish the death penalty, he warned, and groups such as RAM would be free to carry out their threats without fear of capital punishment.

The Wagner pronouncement infuriated Cleveland's black leadership. Staid and moderate middle-class black clergymen who had never before raised their voices in protest were moved to demand a meeting with Mayor Locher. When the Mayor refused to see them they demonstrated with a sit-in at his office. Their prompt arrests and jailings instead of intimidating them merely strengthened their resistance. It was May 1965 when undisguised hatred of Mayor Locher and his policies sprang aflame in Cleveland's black ghettos.

Youngsters, with little to look forward to except the excitement of riotous destructiveness, had no qualms whatever of declaring their intentions of "turning Cleveland upside down and blowing whitey's mind." While their frustration was clearly understood by older people in the black community, it was the older group who decided that its own action and not those of the youngsters would have to dominate the black protest. So little groups of mature black citizens began to hold informal luncheon and dinner meetings at the Lancer Restaurant on Carnegie Avenue. There they began to look at the "mess" into which Cleveland had fallen.

Located near a Cleveland rat exterminating plant, the Lancer is operated by a black man who insists that his predominantly black customers conduct themselves as ladies and gentlemen, when they patronize his establishment. And it was in this strict and orderly atmosphere that Mayor Locher's attitude toward Cleveland's black citizens came under thoughtful reviewing and a thorough roasting. Mayor Locher, an American of Romanian descent was, it seemed, too inclined to please the immigrant Eastern Europeans. And the latter had made their antiblack feelings all too clear.

Moreover, the city fathers were not even listening to black complaints and it was high time they be replaced. The logical place to start was at the top. Cleveland would have to install a responsible and a trustworthy black man in City Hall. But who would he be?

The Lancer lunchers finally hit upon three lawyers. One was Clarence Holmes, President of the Cleveland branch of the N.A.A.C.P., others were Leo A. Jackson, Councilman of the 24th Ward, and Carl B. Stokes, State Representative. They were high on Holmes, but they had to eliminate him almost immediately because they knew his N.A.A.C.P. activities had alienated the white community and a measure of white support was necessary to victory. Jackson was honest enough, but when excited was likely, they believed, to tip over the egg basket. So they focused on Stokes. Yes, he seemed to be the man for black voters and he would appeal to many white voters, too. Stokes was thirty-eight, suave, college-trained, and traveled.

He had an attractive wife and two children. He was a fine speaker, good-looking, a bit inclined to heaviness in the jowls but a little dieting could take care of that in time to launch him on T.V. And that *smile!* Infectious and warm and without the slightest trace of Uncle Tomism that blacks detest in their "leaders." Finally, and this was most vital, Stokes was just the man brothers and sisters at large could easily relate to because he had been through everything familiar to them. His home had been fatherless and his mother had been a domestic on public assistance. Yes, they had their candidate, all right. And they would draft Carl Burton Stokes and run him against Mayor Locher.

But several crucial things went wrong in that 1965 attempt. First, black voter registration was not what it should have been, and Stokes would have to get out the black vote to win. Second, the nine black City Councilmen, deciding in advance that Stokes could not make it against the incumbent Mr. Locher and his majority constituency, were afraid their support of Stokes would be costly to them. So they did not support him. Neither did the influential daily, *The Cleveland Plain Dealer,* nor the powerful labor unions. Still, because Mayor Locher's two terms had been so dismally nonbeneficial to the city, Stokes lost by a mere 2143 votes out of 237,000 cast. The defeated candidate, oddly enough, emerged a more heroic figure than the victor. And the closeness of the vote dictated that Stokes would have to try again.

The Locher third-term victory settled like a foreboding mist over the Cleveland black ghetto. Nowhere was it more oppressive than around the area called Hough. Between 1960 and 1965 the median family income in Hough shrank from $4732 to $3966. And the percentage of families without men to head them swelled from 23 to 32 per cent. Its dilapidated hovels surrounded by the filth in which children played bore testimony to the imminently explosive nature of Hough. It was as if the rotting filth and the rage of those obliged to exist in it were combining to force an eruption. That exactly is what happened. For four humid days and nights Hough residents rioted during the summer of 1966.

Significantly those same Hough residents had been loyal enough to Carl Stokes to hold back their torrent of rage while he was in the running for Mayor a few months before. When Stokes prepared to run again in 1967 the rallying cry in that miserable sector became "Let's cool it for Carl." And the "long hot summer" of 1967 glumly predicted for Cleveland did not materialize. Several forces helped prevent the expected blowup.

When Stokes was about to run in the primary against Locher, black activists of Ohio, who had scheduled a "black unity" rally in Cleveland for September 30 and October 1, suddenly and without explanation called off their plans. Nothing was to detract from this second Stokes effort. Help also came from Atlanta, Georgia. Recalling that Cleveland's black voter registration had not been nearly as high as it should have been when Stokes had run two years previously, Martin Luther King, Jr., entered the picture. During the summer of 1967 he went to Cleveland and appealed to black ghetto youths to keep things cool as he worked there on a voter registration drive. The youngsters, respecting King, did as he asked, with the result that fifty thousand black voters were properly readied for their voting duties in the coming fall.

The Locher forces were infuriated by such aid to black voters. Mayor Locher, himself, declared to the press that he had no intention of meeting with an "extremist" like Martin Luther King, Jr. Even though the black ghetto remained cool during the summer, the Democratic machine backing Locher did all it could to keep the situation hot. It issued campaign newsletters labeling Stokes a "racist Republican," and they exhorted white voters to flock to the polls to "save Cleveland." The tactics of the Fayette, Mississippi, opposition to Charles Evers Mayoral race were never more vicious than those of Stokes' opposition in Cleveland. But they were not to succeed. On October 3, Stokes defeated Locher in the primary with ninety-three thousand black and seventeen thousand white voters. He was now ready to launch his second effort campaign to become Mayor of his native Cleveland, the nation's eighth largest city.

The Republicans, too, had chosen their man. He was

well-to-do forty-four-year-old Seth Taft, scion of a famous
political family and law partner in a powerful Cleveland
firm. As the two candidates swung into their campaigning
each made it clear that race was not the issue upon which
he was seeking to become Mayor. Cleveland voters, however, saw it quite differently. James M. Naughton, political
writer for *The Cleveland Plain Dealer,* made the following observation in his story published in *The New York
Times Magazine* for November 5, 1967:

"There is only one real issue in the campaign. Both
candidates have stated at every opportunity that skin color
is not their concern; so skin color has become the key
concern of the electorate. It all boils down to this issue,
one that has the whole nation on edge: Cleveland must
decide whether its next mayor will be the great-grandson
of a slave or the grandson of President William Howard
Taft."

The Taft headquarters was flooded with calls from irate
white voters complaining that "they're trying to put a
nigger in City Hall." What the callers did not know was
that they were often voicing their fears and hatreds to a
young black woman answering the telephone at the Taft
headquarters. And at one point a member of the Taft team
glumly observed that judging by the way whites were leaving the inner city he'd never live to see another white
Mayor if Stokes won. Many Taft campaign workers were
shocked to learn that their candidate was seeking black
votes. Their shock was matched by that of black voters
equally disdainful of Taft's efforts at wooing and winning
their support. Such was the atmosphere in which both
Stokes and Taft were obliged to present themselves and
their programs to Cleveland voters.

Candidate Taft knew that he could carry the majority
of white voters. But since the margin between the black
and white electorate did not exceed 12 per cent he had to

be sure of that margin. Though he was not appealing to the bigoted white voter, he knew he could count on him. At the same time Seth Taft knew he would have to convince black voters that his running against a black man did not automatically make him a bigot. He was hampered also by a privileged background that ill-prepared him to grasp the intensity of frustrated black feelings.

To Taft's credit, however, he had a basic personal integrity that would not let him patronize or pander to what a lesser white candidate would suppose black voters would want to hear him say. Nor did the Taft family name have any appeal to organized labor in a city traditionally Democratic and anticorporate Republicanism. Labor bitterly recalled that it was Mr. Taft's uncle who had co-authored the hated Taft-Hartley Act.

Stokes, assuming that he could reasonably expect to carry practically the entire black vote, had to have some white support to win. He contemplated the white working men of Hungarian, Polish, Romanian extraction and he pondered how they were torn between their loyalty to pro-labor Democrats and to their lily-white concepts of orderly government. Those were the votes Carl Stokes had to woo. He had no illusions about winning any considerable number of such votes. Neither organized labor nor the local Democratic organization had extended themselves for Carl Stokes. Still, it was up to him to get whatever white labor support he could in spite of not having powerful organizational help.

He began by having a breakfast meeting with the editors of the foreign language newspapers read by those Clevelandites with roots in Eastern Europe. The Stokes charm was never more contagious. On the following day he was editorially endorsed on the front page of the Hungarian daily, *Szabadsag*. That daily declared that under Stokes' leadership, "all of us could live up to the ideals that inspired the ethnic groups to settle in Cleveland in their search for freedom and in the pursuit of happiness."

Candidate Stokes did not fail to tell those "ethnic" whites of his own poverty, of his mother's struggles. He said, "My mother raised me and my brother with the argument that if you study hard, you've got to become somebody. *I know every European immigrant parent told his children the same thing!*"

Stokes had strong white opposition. Those recalling his former support of the N.A.A.C.P.'s and the Urban League's open occupancy fight in local housing, fired loaded questions. How would he handle black "militants"? He replied tersely that H. Rap Brown "would not be welcome in Cleveland" under Mayor Stokes, and he told a black club that he would brook no riots in his town. To a group of all-white policemen he made it clear that as Mayor he would fire Police Chief Richard Wagner as soon as he was installed in City Hall.

The Stokes campaign was doing well enough without dealing with too many specifics until, during a debate, Stokes declared that if Taft won, it would be due to bigotry on the part of white Clevelanders. It was an error for which the opposition had been wishing and waiting. The black candidate, they cried, was showing an arrogance unbecoming a man aspiring to the city's highest office. The Stokes popularity began to wane. But there was still a month to go and Carl Stokes began to settle down to a discussion of serious issues.

He promised to strengthen the police patrol-car force by one third, to eliminate a particularly acute traffic bottleneck, and to enlarge the airport. And he announced plans for an inaugural ball that would raise money for clothing for children of welfare families. He continued, meanwhile, to make personal appearances, to be gentlemanly with his opponent, and to exude his abundance of personal charm. Local white aid came to him by way of campaign money from millionaire industrialist Cyrus Eaton, and the editorial support of *The Cleveland Plain Dealer*. Volunteer workers from the affluent Cleveland suburb of Shaker Heights did help ease mounting difficulties.

Certainly not the least of the latter was a last-minute snowfall that swirled off Lake Erie and lasted mainly all of Election Day. Black poll-watchers, fearful that the weather would keep their southern-born constituents home, uttered silent and not-too-silent prayers. There was fear also that voting machines would confuse the unsophisticated, causing them either to stay home or to vote for the opposing candidate. Earliest returns, giving Taft a lead of three to one, sustained the black community's worst fears. Then as the Taft lead began to ebb, guarded optimism took over until the final votes were counted at 3:30 A.M. Stokes had 129,829; Taft 127,328. Ninety-six per cent of the black and 19 per cent of the white voters had edged him into office.

The jubilation of the Stokes supporters was matched by the graciousness of Mrs. Taft, who presented Mrs. Stokes with a bouquet of roses. In a brief statement Stokes expressed his gratitude for the victory. "It's difficult to tell you what this expression of support, this realization of everything that's wonderful in this wonderful country of ours means to us tonight."

The Mayor-elect looked toward the massive job ahead. Among his first acts were the naming of a new Police Chief, a Safety Director, and a Police Prosecutor. All were white. And the new Mayor ordered his police department to discard the riot helmets that had become a symbol of hostile armed might during the Hough riots.

The demands on Mayor Carl Stokes have been prodigious. Writer James M. Naughton in a second study for

Carl B. Stokes

The New York Times Magazine, February 25, 1969, put it plainly and bluntly. He said:
"Stokes is being judged not as just another new Democratic mayor. He is being judged as a new Negro mayor. He is under more intense scrutiny than any of his predecessors. It matters little in Cleveland that any new mayor faces problems that have crunched atop one another for much of this century without having been solved. Carl Stokes now has the responsibility of trying to solve them. Perhaps sincerely, so soon in the game, black Cleveland wants and white Cleveland demands proof of progress. In 100 days there has not been much; it is questionable whether anyone could have done much so soon."

After his first two months in office Stokes took thirteen days off to recuperate from his strenuous campaign. Had he deliberately sought to pick the most unfortunate time he could find to relax in the Virgin Islands, he could not have been more successful. One of his aides, Geraldine Williams, whose organizational skills had helped put him in office, came under public fire. Mrs. Williams was declared by the Cleveland press to have had a somewhat hazy connection with a club charged with violating the state liquor laws. The case broke while Stokes was out of town and he summarily dismissed Mrs. Williams.

Because Geraldine Williams is black, the local white racists were in high glee. "Didn't we tell you so?" they chortled. On the other hand there were those blacks who had voted for "Soul Brother Carl" with the expectation that he would go easy on errant "brothers and sisters" on his staff. They were furious. "Man, you see *that?*" they cried. "He went right ahead and fired that poor woman just like a *white* man would have done. Didn't even give her a chance to *explain!*" Stokes countered by saying that his administration had ramifications far beyond himself personally, that he was not free to do as he would personally often prefer.

The next thing that happened in the Mayor's first absence from the city was the arrival of an unusually heavy snowstorm. It was a storm that snarled traffic and threw the city's business activity into a state of snowbound confusion. Again the critics cried out. Those who were most critical seemed to take the view that the black Mayor had darkly conspired with the elements to have the storm descend upon Cleveland *after* he had departed for the tropics. One irate merchant presented the city with a bill for $2000 which he had paid a contractor for removing snow piled on the street in front of his establishment.

Then there was the unfortunate case of William Stein, a white professional who had been hired by Stokes to bring City Hall together with state and national heads. Mr. Stein became embroiled in a domestic fracas involving someone's wife and before it was over he received a bullet wound and a lot of uncomplimentary publicity. The Mayor had to fire him also. Those were the imponderables—the unforeseen problems that plague the career of most administrative officials. In addition, Stokes also inherited the specific problems that had tortured Cleveland's Mayors before him.

As he had campaigned on the slogan "Let's do Cleveland proud," he had assured voters that "we don't need a lot of expensive new surveys, studies, reports, and committees. What we need is action. Immediate action!" He had promised to "slash the red tape and flash the green light for urban renewal." Really to do that means that Stokes will have to rid his city's urban renewal department of those who had received their jobs as political pay-offs before he had ever been nominated. And that is no easy job.

Included in the plan for Cleveland's urban renewal are a new downtown bank building and a new luxury downtown hotel, the city's first in half a century. Stokes has managed to clear the way for the former by securing Federal approval, something Mayor Locher was unable to do. As to the new hotel, the possibilities seem greater than they have been in some time.

But the acute shortage in low- and middle-income housing and the shortage of money are still very real to Cleveland. Since the money will have to be raised locally, Stokes has had to break a campaign pledge not to double the city income tax from one half per cent to a flat one per cent. Meanwhile city workers began to demand more pay, which Stokes promised. Again the Mayor's luck was not good. The money he was counting on giving the workers was not tucked away in a former budget as he had been told it was. Surely Stokes can morally disclaim responsibility for inaccurate information given him by others. Still, he knows that as Mayor he will have to come up with suitable solutions to the problems of his city workers.

A particularly annoying problem is the feud with his police department. Stokes did keep a campaign promise to combat the city's rising crime rate by putting more patrolmen on the streets. However, following the assassination of Martin Luther King, Jr., in the spring of 1968, a violent riot again erupted in the black ghetto. Cleveland's white police and its white citizens as well were angered when Stokes ordered the former out of the riot area so that things could cool off. Frustration blended with their anger as the Stokes' stratagem worked.

What they could not apprehend as clearly as their black Mayor was how deeply wounded the rioting Hough residents were by King's murder. It made no favorable impression upon most whites that King had come to Hough earlier and helped its residents discover the power of the vote. But it meant everything to poor blacks when King made the trip from Atlanta to Cleveland to help their very own Carl Stokes make it to City Hall. So word of Dr. King's murder had roused their fury and sent them on a rampage.

The dispatching of white policemen to force them into submissive quiet was not a logical act. But this astute maneuver of their black Mayor, who held authority over the entire city and its predominantly white police force, was. And it was an answer to which they could (and did) respond.

Came November of 1969 and it was time again for the voters to select a Mayor. Again they preferred Carl Stokes to his Republican rival, Ralph J. Perk. The voting turnout was relatively light among both black and white citizens and this time the incumbent Mr. Stokes made even greater inroads into the white community. Again he proved he could triumph in a contest whose prize was a major American city in desperate need of vigorous leadership.

With the second Stokes Mayoral term under way the ills of the ailing city are still in need of tending. The usual pattern of big city crime, illegal gambling, dope smuggling, and prostitution has not vanished from the city simply because Carl Stokes is Mayor. Crimes of violence, common to all deprived areas of large cities, still trouble Clevelanders. Mugging, murders, rape, drunkenness, and the use of narcotics are present and they receive the expected splashy news headlines. And Carl Stokes' troubles with his police department grew bigger and bigger. News of it broke upon the national scene early in 1970.

It happened following a long-smoldering feud between Cleveland's Safety Director and the Chief of Police. Stokes had to replace both. He chose for his Director of Safety retired Air Force Lieutenant General Benjamin O. Davis, Jr. General Davis, son of a career soldier, is the highest ranking black officer in the U. S. Armed Forces. Because he is "all soldier" with an impeccable record of integrity there has been no criticism of the appointment. But the naming of the new Police Chief, William P. Ellenberg, was another matter. Mr. Ellenberg, it was charged, had allegedly been on the Mafia payroll when he was in Detroit. So intense was public pressure on Chief Ellenberg that he resigned and Stokes was obliged to explain how he happened to slip up on this particular appointment.

The Cleveland Plain Dealer that had supported Stokes' two elections rapped him firmly in a front-page editorial. Wrote editor-publisher Thomas Vail: "Time is running out. The people of Cleveland will not stand for another fiasco in public safety."

Carl Stokes, the charming politician, who rose from the slums of Cleveland to become the first black Mayor of a major American city, is a man besieged. His is not an enviable position. Yet, he wanted it badly enough to fight racism in its many forms to attain it. Perhaps he will be a stronger man for having had it. Perhaps not. It is certain, however, that Cleveland and the nation have done much for themselves that is good for having put him where he is.

Richard Gordon Hatcher

It WAS THE MORNING of May 15, 1969, and the Mayor of Gary, Indiana, was holding his biweekly Thursday breakfast meeting at the Hotel Gary. The meeting was, as usual, open to any citizen who wished to come and listen and comment upon the subject to be discussed. Coffee and donuts were served and the meeting, starting promptly at eight-thirty, ran for a bit more than thirty minutes. The subject at this particular meeting was summer employment opportunities for Gary's youth.

Of the forty or so assembled citizens nearly half were black. Several of them obviously were parents of young people who would be needing summer work. When he had introduced the subject and revealed the city's plans for employing workers, the Mayor entertained questions. Following the first two questions, the dicussion veered sharply from the announced subject as an articulate, well-groomed white citizen rose to speak.

He said: "Mr. Mayor, I've just recently returned from Cleveland, Ohio, where I observed how amicably the two races are getting along. The people with whom I talked seemed so pleased with Mayor Stokes and the wonderful things he is doing for Cleveland. Upon returning home I

was sadly reminded of all the strife we have here and I've
been wondering why we in Gary have to do so poorly—
especially in our race relations."

The speaker's tone was modulated and one detected the
wisp of a smile around his mouth as he sat down. Mayor
Hatcher responded with cool and controlled politeness:
"We have an interesting coincidence here. I too have just
returned from Cleveland and from what you have just said
it is hard to believe we saw the same city. Surely we did
not talk to the same people. I talked with Carl Stokes,
among others, and from what he told me I am certain he is
most anxious to locate those Clevelanders who are doing so
nicely with their race relations."

When the laughter subsided, the Mayor explained that
no city has a monopoly on virtuous or sinful citizens. He
further said that while the neighbor's pasture usually appears greener and more attractive than one's own, there
are always those problems that one knows about only when
he has full access to total information.

Another neatly dressed white citizen cited the "lack of
love" between Gary's black and white citizens. He had
heard and seen Charles Evers on T.V. and was convinced
that Evers was "far greater than Martin Luther King, Roy
Wilkins, and Whitney Young combined." His reason?
Evers' brand of talk, he concluded, promoted brotherly
love. Again the Mayor's response was controlled and tinged
with good humor. If he was annoyed he gave no sign of it,
for that is the kind of man he is.

These two brief exchanges reflected a common difficulty
too many people experience in trying to deal normally and
comfortably with others whose race happens to differ from
theirs. It revealed how Mayor Hatcher was not permitted
to communicate for as little as thirty minutes with his fellow citizens on a subject not directly related to race. Two
men could not refrain from revealing that they saw a black

man addressing them. But the Mayor was not there to explain blackness and its relation to whiteness. He was there to discuss summer job possibilities for Gary's youth.

Just how many others in the room reacted similarly to Mayor Hatcher, without voicing their feelings, no one can know for certain. But one does know that unsheathed racism had completely split Gary immediately before and during the Hatcher victory. The records reveal the Gary Mayoral contest of 1967 as one of the bitterest and most astounding in this nation's history.

Richard Gordon Hatcher is a dark-brown man of medium height and build. Unless you knew him or unless you were particularly observant you would pass him on the street without giving him a second glance. Upon closer inspection, however, you notice that he grooms himself with exquisite care and yet he doesn't make his grooming conspicuous. When he shakes your hand you become ever so slightly aware of the physical power of the athlete that he has been. His healthy skin and hair reflect his abstinence from tobacco and alcohol; and, but for a defect in his left eye, he appears to be a near-perfect physical specimen. "Clean-cut," that much-abused description, fits him well.

It is when he speaks, however, that you notice something distinctly special about him. He wastes no words. Nor does he make use of the meaningless cliches and platitudes that invade the speech of so many politicians. Richard Hatcher, when he speaks, has something to say.

Born on July 10, 1933, in Michigan City, Indiana, Richard was one of a large family. The Hatcher children were born and reared in a section of Michigan City called The Patch. Over the years The Patch decayed to the point where it had to be replaced by a public housing project. Most of its residents were black. As is true of ghetto residents, those who were self-respecting and decent shared the area's misery with those involved in crime and other degrading activities.

During Richard's earliest years his father, Carlton Hatcher, worked in a factory—whenever he could find work. Those were the years of the depression. As Richard began to develop, his mother, Catherine Hatcher, went out to work also, leaving the children rather on their own. Life was not easy for the Hatchers, but they were a close-knit family with a strong attachment to their church. Mrs. Hatcher was a faithful member of the Church of God in Christ and she never failed to take Richard to the services with her. Later he was to join the Mount Zion Baptist Church of which his father, Carlton, was a stanch member. So from those early lean years as a regular churchgoer and from the closest kind of contact with his deeply religious parents, Richard developed his code of ethical conduct. It was a code that has motivated him to stand firm for that which he believes is just and right.

Richard was a normally lively and healthy boy who enjoyed romping and racing with other children. It was during such boys' play that a playmate accidently threw a stone that struck Richard in the eye. He was only eight or nine and Catherine Hatcher resolved then and there that Richard would have to get a good education. A man with one eye, she reasoned, would be no good as a factory worker. So Richard, always interested in learning, liked school. Though small and wiry he enjoyed sports, for at Michigan City's Elston High School he performed well as a high jumper and sprinter, though less successfully as a football player.

He was fourteen when his mother died. Her death was a loss Richard felt deeply for a long time, though his father soon remarried, and his stepmother came as close as anyone could to being a real mother. His mother's death, it seemed, created in Richard a particular sensitiveness to life in The

Patch. The meanness of the existence he knew so well there occupied much of his thinking. So as a high school student it was natural that Richard would gravitate toward those school groups seeking to better conditions of the poor, especially poor blacks.

Carlton Hatcher recalls with a measure of paternal pride that his son was "sent home several times from school for expressing opinions too openly." Says the elder Hatcher:

"He kept his brother-in-law Emmett Wise and myself quite busy going to school with him to get things 'straightened out.' When Richard thought something was wrong he was not afraid to say so."

Richard was fifteen and a part-time restaurant dishwasher when his employer infuriated him by refusing to serve a party of orderly black patrons. He said what he felt he had to say about discrimination and promptly quit his job.

Richard finished high school with a creditable record. With the help of an athletic scholarship, a small church grant, help from older brothers and sisters, he enrolled at the University of Indiana. There he worked after school hours as a waiter and majored in economics and government. Meanwhile he began to develop what was to become an extraordinary skill at public speaking. Following graduation in 1956 from the University of Indiana, Richard moved on to Valparaiso University in pursuit of a degree in law. For the next three years he attended classes from 8:30 A.M. to 3:30 P.M., then worked the 4 P.M. to midnight shift in a hospital. Studying came in between. Despite the grueling schedule, he obtained his law degree, graduating with honors in criminal law. It was 1959 when he began the private practice of law in East Chicago, Indiana. At the same time he opened a second law office in Gary. His first job in politics was as a deputy prosecutor in the Lake County Criminal Court. There he worked obscurely until 1963, when he ran for the City Council as a Democrat without party machine help. Hatcher surprised the old-line politicians by polling 12,799 votes, the largest number ever received by a Councilman-at-large.

Within a year he, Gary's youngest City Councilman, became that body's President. With this advantage, Hatcher quickly established his stand for an open occupancy housing ordinance, paving the way for integrated housing. And he began to acquaint himself with other urban problems. Among them were taxes and air pollution—knowledge that was to help him immeasurably in his later Mayoral campaign. In his honest and youthful enthusiasm it is doubtful that Richard Hatcher, with all his keen intelligence, fully apprehended the harsh character of the city he had chosen to work in.

Gary is a smoke-shrouded steel city of 180,000 people. Its huge mills produce more steel than those at Pittsburgh. The bulk of its working population earn their living in the mills operated by that industrial colossus, the United States Steel Corporation. Gary, next-door neighbor of Chicago, has its foreign language groups, representing mainly the ethnic groups of middle Europe. They look with apprehension and suspicion upon the largest single ethnic group, the black Americans, who comprise slightly more than half the city's population.

United States Steel had built the city on the southern tip of Lake Michigan in 1906. Then it had brought in the Croats, Serbs, Czechs, Hungarians, Slovaks, Greeks, and Italians to do the harsh dirty work. The first black workers did not arrive until after World War I. They were imported from the south by United States Steel to break a strike. The European immigrant steelworkers have never forgotten that early threat to their existence posed by those hungry black strike-breaking refugees from Mississippi, Alabama, Louisiana, Arkansas, and Texas. To this day Gary's white immigrants remain hostile to Gary's black migrants.

So when Hatcher came upon the scene the black workers, though numerically stronger, held only a trifle more than one fourth of the jobs, and those were of the low-paying variety. Worse still, the black workers had been forced to live in an area of Gary measuring a trifle more than six and a half of the city's fifty-six square miles.

Political corruption and its companion, police corruption, permitted such unbridled organized crime and vice as to give Gary the label "Sin City of the Midwest." Mobs controlled the rackets that yielded three hundred million dollars each year in gambling, loansharking, and prostitution. Anything that was profitably illegal was for many years sanctioned in Gary, Indiana. And public officials not actively engaged in the various illegalities were "persuaded" to look the other way. The record of a few of the city's former Mayors reads like comic page fiction.

Gary's first Mayor, Tom Knotts, elected in 1906, was arrested fourteen times for corruption during his first two years in office. A later Mayor, Daryl Johnson, served four years in prison, came out and was re-elected Mayor. An even more recent Mayor, who had served three years in the Federal Penitentiary, was to turn up in the camp of the man against whom Hatcher would run for the city's top office.

Next to United States Steel, the Democratic political machine was Gary's second largest employer. Such was the climate of Gary that Council President Richard Gordon Hatcher decided it had to be changed. The raw bone-chilling enormity of the task never seemed to bother him. When it became known that he aimed to be Mayor of Gary someone quickly asserted that Hatcher had lived in the city only seven years and, moreover, he was far too young. Councilman Hatcher's retort was typical of him: "I got here as fast as I could."

The first step toward City Hall was through the spring

primary contest of 1967, and that was where Hatcher headed. But a funny thing happened on the way to the primary. Someone offered Hatcher $100,000 if he would not enter and he refused to accept the offer. Cynical mobsters and political machine hacks were aghast. What ailed Richard Hatcher? How could this poor young black man turn his back on a fortune he could scarcely hope to earn honestly? *Every* man has his price, so what on earth did Hatcher want? What *was* this, anyway?

When it became apparent that the young Councilman was in earnest, the opposition to him reached a fever pitch. Headed by John G. Krupa, powerful Chairman of the Lake County Democratic Party, the machine put the weight of its influence behind incumbent Mayor A. Martin Katz. And Hatcher promptly challenged the record of his opponent. Though he admitted that Mayor Katz had probably been fairer to Gary's black citizens than any Mayor before him, Hatcher posed a few pointed questions:

"I ask you, are the slums any prettier? Have they torn down a single building for urban renewal? Have they built a single housing project? Have they expanded the park system? Have they desegregated the schools? Are our schools any less crowded?"

Mayor Katz's reply was to brand Hatcher "a radical extremist and advocate of black power." In tones grim and full of foreboding he warned that Hatcher's election would bring an end to law and order, that Gary would become a battlefield, with blacks terrorizing the entire city. The press immediately questioned Hatcher on black power and learned that he favored the pooling of resources over burning and looting as a means of improving conditions in the black ghetto. Still the regular local Democrats would not support Democrat Hatcher, nor would the local news media publish anything about him that might bring votes his way.

But Hatcher had friends outside Gary. Because he had

no money to finance an elaborate primary campaign, Harry Belafonte went twice to Gary and staged two fund-raising benefits for him. In addition, two nationally prominent Democrats, Hubert H. Humphrey and the late Robert F. Kennedy, lent the prestige of their names to the Hatcher cause, though they did little campaigning. In the May primary voting Hatcher polled 20,272 votes to 17,190 for Katz. His victory was due mainly to a splitting of the white vote by a segregationist candidate who took votes from Katz. Fewer than twelve hundred of the winner's tallies came from white voters. Hatcher had achieved the near impossible.

On the other side of the political line Joseph B. Radigan, college dropout and owner of an inherited furniture store business, had won the Republican primary. Mr. Radigan, in his first try for public office, had received a small but winning majority of 3846 votes. It would appear on the surface that the Democratic candidate would win in a walk-away. Had he been white such would have been the case. But the contest began, from the moment the primary was over, to form itself into the dirtiest and most bitter in Gary's sordid political history.

Mayor Katz made a public show of loyalty to the Democratic Party by publicly endorsing Hatcher. However, many of his department heads wore Radigan buttons. Then the Democratic City Council, with Hatcher dissenting, cut the jobs of two vital aides to the Mayor from the coming year's budget. They were out to cripple the city's operation under a probable Hatcher administration.

The Hatcher forces, two thousand volunteers strong and guided by campaign manager Henry Coleman, went from door to door to register eligible voters. Their "Operation Saturation" caught fire with the black working class but made little impression upon black politicians and clergy-men. The latter were convinced Hatcher could not win. So also were those Gary whites who had voted strongly for Alabama Governor George Wallace in the 1964 Presidential primary.

But "Operation Saturation" captured the attention of pudgy, Democratic Chairman John Krupa. Krupa, a super-patriot of Polish descent, was ever on the alert for Communist subversives. Never shy about offering advice, he had previously cautioned Hatcher against a tendency among black Americans toward "impatience." "The trouble with you people is you're not willing to wait your turn," he had declared. And with an I-know-what's-best-for-you-people attitude he agreed to back Hatcher under one condition. He, Krupa, and the organization would have to select the Chief of Police and other key city officials after a Hatcher victory. Hatcher replied that too many people had put too much in the effort to be sold out. No, he alone would select his own Police Chief and Controller.

Stung by the rebuff, Krupa called upon Hatcher to publicly repudiate Martin Luther King, Jr., Stokely Carmichael, Joan Baez, H. Rap Brown, and Marlon Brando. They along with other Americans had sponsored a "peace" ad in *The London Times* and they were, in Krupa's view, dangerous and destructive tools of Communism. Again Hatcher refused the Krupa demand. Within a matter of days Krupa had distributed a reprint of a supposed Hatcher interview in the Black Muslim newspaper, *Muhammad Speaks.* Hatcher in the interview was "quoted" as having suggested that captured American pilots in Vietnam should be treated by Hanoi as war criminals. The paper's retraction of this Hatcher story was never mentioned by Krupa. Shortly thereafter the area in and around Gary was plastered with Red, White, and Blue billboards proclaiming Mr. Radigan's 100 per cent Americanism. The inference that Hatcher, surrounded by subversives, was not a loyal American was not wasted on frightened voters.

Hatcher then tried reason. He said: "I am certain I will get a lot of votes from prostitutes, but it is obviously unfair to hold me responsible for their attitudes or willingness to break the law."

But the "red" and "pink" labels were very real to many white voters, whose chilly reception of Hatcher as he toured shopping centers was all too evident. Many refused to shake his hand. Hatcher tried the shock treatment on especially hostile audiences.

He told them: "I know you haven't heard a word I said. All you see in front of you is black. But if by some miracle, race was ruled out, and I and my opponent were considered only on qualifications, the election wouldn't even be close. All my opponent talks about is that he comes from an old family, long established in Gary. He says he's been in the furniture business forty-seven years. I want to see that he stays there."

Sabotage against Hatcher within the local Democratic organization continued, as Krupa refused to appoint Deputy Election Commissioners in black precincts. In such precincts voter registration was seriously crippled. And about five thousand black voters who had profited by the rackets went out under syndicate orders to work against Hatcher. Prominent white support for him, however, was not totally absent. Indianapolis Congressman Andrew Jacobs, Jr., went directly into Krupa territory and valiantly urged Hatcher's election. But money was running dangerously low. The Hatcher campaign could not look to rich resources for aid.

Then, over the protests of his campaign manager, Hatcher, himself, made a desperate move. He placed a $6690 ad in *The New York Times* under the following heading: FOR GOD'S SAKE LET US GET OURSELVES TOGETHER. The ad did bring small donations sufficient to cover its cost and that was all. It was August and the campaign treasury was empty. Then, miraculously, contributions began to trickle in. By October, $60,000 had been received and it looked as though everything would work out well after all. Then came the boldest of all the enemy attacks against the Hatcher campaign.

Two weeks before the election John Krupa had 5286 names of voters dropped from the registration lists. Most of them were names of black voters. Simultaneously four thousand fictitious or "ghost" names were added to the lists and it was planned that impostors would be paid to assume those "ghost" names and cast votes against Hatcher. But Hatcher, anticipating some desperate scheme to assure his defeat, was ahead of the schemers. He had wired Attorney General Ramsey Clark requesting a Justice Department examination of the situation. There was but one week to go before election. Again Hatcher, using his legal experience, went to Federal Court and charged the Krupa forces with violating the Voting Rights Act of 1965.

With the eyes of the nation now on Gary, both of Indiana's Democratic Senators demanded Federal investigation of the Hatcher charges. Within forty-eight hours the 5286 names that had disappeared from the registration lists suddenly reappeared. Nevertheless, Attorney General Clark sent twenty-two F.B.I. agents to Gary to check the alleged irregularities. What they found and uncovered shocked even the most crime-hardened Gary voters. The most dramatic and shocking exposure came from precinct committeewoman Marion Tokarski. Mrs. Tokarski, who had served the Democratic Party for twelve years, tearfully admitted to fraud in her all-white precinct. She personally had added fifty-one fraudulent names to registration rolls and, as she explained, she could not live in peace with the knowledge of her guilt. Besides, she declared she was finally convinced that Hatcher was not a Communist as she had previously been led to believe. Mrs. Tokarski's testimony, coming just hours before the polls opened, stirred rumors of violence in some white neighborhoods. The entire Gary police force went on a twelve-hour shift and Governor Branigin prepared three hundred state troopers and five thousand National Guardsmen to move into the city on his orders. Gary was like a time bomb waiting to be detonated.

The polls opened for what turned out to be the most peaceful of all the city's elections. And, thanks to Hatcher's alertness and the equally alert Federal intervention, it was also quite probably one of the fairest elections in many years. With a record turnout, and with black voters casting solidly for Hatcher, the final count placed Hatcher ahead of Radigan by a scant margin of 1389 votes. Hatcher, a bachelor and thirty-four, took office as Gary's first black Mayor.

The new Mayor wasted no time. He appointed James F. Hilton, a white officer who has the respect of the entire city, as Police Chief. Within six weeks most of the major gambling and prostitution activities went out of business. One black restauranteur who had been conducting a gambling operation and selling unlicensed liquor in the basement of his establishment paid Hatcher a call. He had, he asserted, contributed heavily to the Hatcher campaign and had come to see what "consideration" he would get for his effort. He was unceremoniously told to get out and clean up his business before he was closed up and jailed.

Street crimes in Gary, however, committed mostly by unemployed youth, did not suddenly fall off. Nor did the construction of public housing projects for blacks in predominantly white areas begin quickly as planned. To correct these two deficiencies the Mayor sought more rapid-moving employment and housing programs for the deprived. To this end he did not hesitate to enlist the aid of the local business community as well as the Federal government. Still white opposition to public housing in white neighborhoods remained stubborn. And black expectations that "their Mayor" could work miracles in a few weeks were certainly not realistic.

By the end of 1968 Hatcher was able to report that his visits to white areas of the city were no longer experiences in near total unpleasantness. "People almost spat on me before," he says. "That's how strong the feeling was. Today I hear mothers tell their children, 'Here's the Mayor, get his autograph.'" Mayor Hatcher quickly adds that there are "still many people in the city who can't bring themselves to accept the fact that Gary has a black Mayor." And he explains that many others are cooperating not because they love him but because they recognize their stake in the city. "If it goes down they go down with it."

The Mayor takes a degree of pride in the fact that Gary's severe housing crisis is undergoing a change for the better. Of the $30 million in Federal aid received during his first year, $12 million was from the Department of Housing and Rehabilitation. The city's redesigned building department has rewritten all of Gary's housing and building codes, to the advantage of tenants. Building permits are no longer loosely issued to contractors who in the past failed to account in detail for the fees they received. Buildings abandoned by landlords because they are health and safety hazards are boarded up. Bills for their repair are then issued to the owners by the city. And whenever a landlord refuses to repair an occupied unsafe building, the city takes it over, collects the rents, and uses the monies for necessary repairs.

Operation Showcase selects a city block as a model to show what can be done with local resources. Where painting is needed and that block's residents cannot afford to buy paint, the city supplies it. If garbage pickups must be accelerated to keep that block's alleys clean, the city sees that more pickups are made. Inspectors are constantly probing the block to see what improvements need to be made, prompting block residents to take greater pride and interest in their area.

With typical Hatcher directness the Mayor has attacked the need for jobs with his Concentrated Employment Program (CEP). Using Federal funds, he has enrolled over a thousand unemployed persons in job training activities. There is, for example, Soul Incorporated. This group of jobless youths, many with prison and jail records, were put to work operating their own skating rink and community center. Even the United States Steel Corporation has relaxed its high school diploma requirement so that hard-core jobless youths may be hired. That is not all. In addition to paying them for their work, the company pays them for so many hours per working day to attend school.

Hatcher was able in his first year as Mayor to get additional cooperation from Gary's business community. The Gary National Bank has made $2 million available as loans to ghetto residents who want to set up or to expand businesses. The Metropolitan Life Insurance Company has set aside an equal amount of mortgage money where none was previously available. A gift of 145 acres of land from United States Steel will provide a park and a small boat harbor, and the same company began the building of five hundred units of middle income housing.

The elimination of Gary's organized crime already mentioned is due primarily to Mayor Hatcher's special task force. This group of thirteen men is answerable only to the Mayor, his Police Chief, and the Assistant Police Chief. The formation of this unit enables the city to deal effectively with policemen carried over from previous administrations who could be neither trusted nor fired. Unorganized crime—robberies, muggings, and offenses less easily dealt with—are constantly under attack by another Hatcher unit, a sixteen-man tactical force headed by the Assistant

Chief of Police. Most significant in this connection is the Mayor's insistence that crimes of all kinds be treated with equally just concern. Crimes committed by blacks against blacks in the past were not regarded as seriously as crimes committed by blacks against whites. Mayor Hatcher will brook no such "jim crow justice." At the same time he is fully cognizant of the breadth of his duties as Mayor. As he has publicly declared:

"I am the Mayor of Gary and, thus, I am the Mayor of all the people of the city, and I would like to do my best for all of them, black or white. But, you know, what I cannot do for black brothers, I cannot do for white people either, try as I might. The black community needs are infinitely greater, but the white community in our city is not without its problems. For the same reasons which prevent me from solving many of the black problems, I cannot solve many of the white ones either. Neither could my white predecessors."

Hatcher freely admits the difficulties that plagued his first year in office: "In July 1968 we experienced civil disorder that was characterized in some quarters of the public press as a 'riot.' But what we experienced was not a riot, despite the usually long-distance clairvoyant assessments of some who reported the events. It demonstrated, however, that Gary is not immune to civil disturbances just because it has a black Mayor. He, too, must deal with the root causes of such disturbances."

There were strikes in Gary during the new Mayor's first year and they were astutely brought under control.

The most difficult of Hatcher's problems as Mayor has been his City Council, which, for many reasons, has been an obstacle to many of his new programs. He has concluded that there is a kind of natural hostility between the legislative and executive branches of government. And he is aware also of racism and the political ambitions of Councilmen. He too was a Councilman with ambitions. But he is not friendly to Councilmen whose ambitions drive them to take positions detrimental to the city. *"That,"* he declares tersely, "I *do* mind." Most trying of all his problems with some Councilmen, however, is their insistence that the traditional system of political patronage that operated so freely in Gary in the past is quite good and proper for Gary now. To those Councilmen, Hatcher, a strict believer in the merit system, is an alien. But alien or not, Hatcher, exercising his belief in merit, chose a new Chief of Police early in 1970. He is thirty-nine-year-old Charles Boone, a veteran of thirteen years' experience. Chief Boone is the fifth black man in Gary to hold one of the city's top positions. Others are the Fire Chief, City Attorney, and City Controller. Even though the Mayor made the appointments only after the most careful consideration, they have not pleased the majority of the city's white population.

Finally there has been the Mayor's relationship with the press. Nationally he seems to do well. The New York, Chicago, and Washington newspapers have generally printed positive news about Gary. Locally he has done less well, and of the Gary press he has had the following to say:

"The local paper emphasizes things like my arriving at a press conference ten minutes late. It doesn't matter that during the press conference I might have announced a multimillion-dollar program for Gary. They downplay that and emphasize my tardiness. The fact that previous Mayors never held press conferences is never mentioned."

Such are the satisfactions and the dissatisfactions of Mayor Richard Gordon Hatcher. He bravely wanted to be Gary's Mayor and, now that he is, he bravely goes about his job with the zeal born of intelligence and honesty. What he strives for as he moves ahead with his program of reform is best expressed in his own words concluding an address he delivered in New York City on February 22, 1969:

"Let us turn the promise of America into real progress; let us turn the dream into reality. For the sake of God, for the sake of man, for the sake of America, let's get ourselves together."

Edward W. Brooke

He is the first black man to sit in the United States Senate in eighty-five years. To designate him "black" outside the United States is to confuse and confound others not familiar with the peculiarly American mode of determining who is and who is not black in America. Many years ago it became an accepted racist dictum in our country that a black person was anyone having in his veins "one drop of black blood." Using that dictum as a guide, Senator Brooke does indeed qualify as black. So also do many Americans not as thoroughly familiar with their antecedents as Edward Brooke is of his.

Senator Brooke fully knows who and what he is. True, his personal style—his dress, speech, and manner—do not shriek, "Yeah, baby, I'm a soul brother too!" Neither, for that matter, do those of Congressman John Conyers of Michigan or N.A.A.C.P. lobbyist Clarence Mitchell who are close associates of the Senator. But whenever any official voice in this country even faintly suggests a denial of black citizens' rights, those three men, along with other black representatives in Washington, speak out in quick and eloquent rebuttal.

In such instances the voice of Senator Brooke is no less

urgent because of his near-white skin or because he was elected to the Senate by a white Massachusetts majority. It could not be otherwise with him. He too knows what it is to be a black man—albeit a member of the black bourgeoisie—in predominantly white America. In an interview published in the *U.S. News & World Report* for February 1, 1965, the newly elected Senator Brooke was asked: "In your own campaign was the race issue raised against you?" He replied, "I have run three times, state-wide, and the racial issue has always been raised."

The son of an attorney employed for years by the Veterans Administration, Edward Brooke was born and reared in Washington, D.C. His ancestry, not unlike that of many black Americans, can be traced to the family relationships that existed between slaves and their owners. Like most black children of his generation, regardless of the whiteness or blackness of their skins, little Edward was constantly reminded by a protective old-fashioned grandmother to "stay in your place." It was the old folks' way of shielding their young from the cruel rebuffs awaiting them out in the white man's world.

Although he grew up in the black community and attended the jim crow schools designated for black Washingtonians, he did manage to escape the added humiliation of material poverty. His mother, Helen Seldon Brooke, saw to it that her two children, Helene (the older) and Edward, enjoyed those modest comforts a gainfully employed government lawyer could afford his family. She wanted them to be "cultivated" in the middle-class interpretation of the term, so she saw to it that they attended concerts and the opera. Since black patrons were, at that time, discriminated against by Washington's theater managers, Helen Brooke took her children to the opera and the theater in New York.

At home in Washington the Brookes attended the segregated but austere St. Luke's Episcopal Church. There, in startling contrast to the whooping and hollering in black Methodist and Baptist churches, the ritual was genteel and "cultured." Services and decorum in black Episcopal churches are carbon copies of those in white churches of the same denomination. Indeed, the membership of most black Episcopal churches prior to World War II was quite noticeably not black in complexion. So, with its fair-skin members and its restrained tone, St. Luke's clung to a pattern established during slavery.

It was a pattern that had created and maintained a gulf between the slaves who were blood relations of their masters and those who were not. The light-skin slaves had the easier chores and though they were made to know they were slaves, they nevertheless thought of themselves as superior to their darker brothers. In their world of make-believe they adopted the airs of their masters. And this was like manna from heaven to the masters, who knew only too well that slaves divided were slaves easily ruled and managed.

Young Brooke attended Washington's all-black Dunbar High School, famous for its uniformed cadet corps and its tradition of having graduated scores of black students who, after college training, entered the professions of medicine, law, and teaching. It was natural that Edward Brooke, following his father's example, would enter predominantly black Howard University. And it was natural that he would seriously entertain thoughts of studying medicine at Howard's famed medical school, since as a high school youth he had shown a marked interest in biology and chemistry. So, during his undergraduate years he majored in chemistry and zoology and, following Howard University's well-known social traditions, he became President of the Alpha Phi Alpha fraternity.

Brooke with his R.O.T.C. training and his bachelor's degree left Howard University in 1941, just in time to be called into the U. S. Army as a second lieutenant. He was assigned to the all-black 366th Combat Infantry Regiment at Fort Devens, Massachusetts. As was customary with young officers, Second Lieutenant Brooke was delegated the task of defending accused enlisted men in both general and special court-martial cases. The alternative would have been for him to act in the capacity of Trial Judge Advocate, but he preferred the role of defender. Before long he had become popular among prisoners, who were anxious to have him defend them. After a quick promotion to First Lieutenant, he was sent to Fort Benning, Georgia, for advanced infantry training. Brooke then returned to Devens to rejoin the 366th Regiment and its 92nd Division, which sailed for combat action in Italy.

Lieutenant Brooke's valor under fire earned for him a Bronze Star. Moreover, his facility with the Italian tongue, added to his swarthy Italian appearance, enabled him to work effectively behind enemy lines with the Italian partisan guerrillas.

Following V. E. Day, Captain Brooke took a vacation in Viareggio on the Ligurian Sea, while awaiting to be sent home. One day while relaxing on the beach he met vivacious brown-eyed Remigia Ferrari-Scacco, daughter of a successful paper merchant. Though they saw each other in Italy only twice, they knew they were in love. Edward asked Remigia to marry him and he even met her parents. But as any well-bred Italian girl would have done, she put him off for a while, though she has since admitted falling in love with him on sight. Edward, already home, kept in touch with Remigia by mail. He had meanwhile to decide upon a career.

Would it be medicine or law? Two buddies who had seen Army service with Brooke helped him make the decision. They were Alfred Brothers and Clarence Elam, who had seen and admired his defense of prisoners at Fort Devens. Both men were convinced that Brooke's field should be law and they told him so. "Why not come to Boston to study and set up your practice?" they urged.

It was the autumn of 1946 when Edward Brooke arrived in Boston to enroll in the Law School at Boston University. Until then all of the twenty-six years of his life had been spent among his own people. He had grown up in a middle-class black neighborhood, gone to segregated public schools and to the nearly all-black Howard University. As an Army officer he had commanded black troops in Italy, leaving them only temporarily as he adopted the role of "Carlo," the Italian guerrilla partisan. Of those early years he says:

"The world of white men was something which I observed only from afar and which I felt no particular desire to be a part of. I know the dreadful discriminations and bigotry which many American Negroes have suffered, but honestly I cannot claim that this had any shattering effect on me."

Now he was attending Law School with whites and was living in a nearby Italian-American settlement. And he was constantly reminded of Remigia. For the next few months they exchanged love letters in her native Italian. When he proposed a second time, this time by mail she accepted, and left Italy for New York almost immediately. She and Brooke were married in Boston in June 1947. They rented an apartment in the Hill section of Roxbury where Malcolm X had come to live with his older sister, Ella. And Ed Brooke settled down to study as he had never done while an undergraduate student at Howard University.

Not unlike other young war veterans, he had a maturity about him now that stimulated him to make a brilliant Law School record. Before graduation in 1948 he was editor of the *Law Review* and by 1950 he had his Master of Law degree. He joined his wartime buddy Al Brothers and together they opened a combination real estate and law office

in Roxbury. Because the partners were in close and constant touch with their mutual pal Clarence Elam, it wasn't
long before they began to think and talk together in terms
of practical politics. Why shouldn't their black 12th Ward
be politically represented by a black man? And why
shouldn't Ed be the one to run for the Legislature?

Although Brooke was surprised by his friends' suggestion
he was by no means offended by it. But how serious could
they be, he wondered? After all, here he was thirty years
old and had never voted! What on earth did he know of
politics? Then there was Remigia. When she heard what
the three had been discussing she nearly collapsed, recalling
the rash of murders of the Italian politicos of her experience under the Mussolini regime. But the initial excitement and anxiety soon wore away and Ed Brooke, neither
a registered Republican nor Democrat, filed for both parties' nominations for State Representative from Roxbury's
12th Ward.

He won the Republican endorsement and has been with
the party ever since. But winning endorsement and winning the election were entirely different things. He was
defeated in the 1950 general election, tried again two years
later and was defeated again. Brooke was disgusted. He was
through with politics, he declared, especially upon hearing
rumors that his defeats were due in part to his marriage to
a white woman. However, he was urged to run for Secretary
of State in 1960. His opponent just happened to be Kevin
White, whose very name offered a tempting weapon to the
racists to use against Brooke. So it surprised no one when
the campaign slogan "Vote White" helped bring about Ed
Brooke's third election defeat.

This time, however, the margin of defeat was so narrow
as to encourage Brooke to keep trying. Besides, there were
new forces at work in Boston—forces seeking to alter the
old pattern of stagnant machine politics. Massachusetts,

traditionally a Democratic state, was, it seemed, the domain of the powerful Kennedy and McCormick clans. The state's politics, often described as "tribal and feudalistic," had for years been under one-party control. Moreover, the Bay State's reputation as one riddled with political corruption is well known throughout the nation.

Long before Edward Brooke entered politics, bribery, theft, conspiracy, and nepotism were rampant. One State Representative had been convicted of larceny and re-elected while still in jail. Massachusetts Democrats were not alone in the commission of crimes, though Republican shenanigans were less extensive. Actually, even before the Democratic rogues attained power the aloof Republican Party had been the preserve of old Yankee Protestant families, until they were toppled by the Democrats. The Republicans saw little chance of regaining their stature until someone viewing the influx of Irish, Italians, and Jews had an idea.

Perhaps they could recapture a measure of their former strength by offering "ethnic" candidates to voters seeking to break with the old tradition of their Democratic rivals. So they tried it. They were able, for instance, in 1960 to rally the Italian vote behind John Volpe, and Mr. Volpe became the first Roman Catholic Republican Governor in Massachusetts' history. Two years later the Republicans used the same strategy. This time they offered three Yankees —an Irishman, an Italian, a Jew—and a black candidate. The latter, nominated for Attorney General, was young attorney Edward Brooke.

During the previous year Governor Volpe had appointed Brooke as Chairman of the Boston Finance Commission. That commission, formed to attack corruption in the various city agencies, was made to order for the young lawyer from Roxbury. With the zeal of a man determined to prove he could do a first-rate job in spite of slurs about his race and his choice of a wife, he tore into his work with fire and gusto.

Before he was through he had exposed flagrant abuses in the sale of city land, resulting in the dismissal of City Auctioneer John J. McGrath. McGrath had been buying city property at "bargain basement" prices he himself had set. Another of Brooke's accomplishments as Commission Chairman was the bringing into Boston of a national expert to examine corruption in the city's police department. This prompt Brooke action followed a previously televised C.B.S. documentary titled "Biography of a Bookie Joint" which showed, among other things, a Boston policeman entering such a place.

Chairman Brooke was establishing the Boston Finance Commission as a body deserving of public respect. Meanwhile he was thinking and looking ahead toward running for the seat of Attorney General. The Brooke decision to seek that office did not, however, induce his liberal Republican backers to leap with joy. Pleased as they were with the headlines he had made as a crusader for clean city government, they had reservations about his newest aims. First, considering his race, they reasoned that registered black Massachusetts voters, numbering less than 2 per cent of the state's electorate, could not put Brooke into office.

They then began to worry about Brooke's rival in the nomination, Elliot Richardson. Mr. Richardson was a millionaire Boston "blueblood" partner in a prominent law firm. A Harvard graduate and former athlete, he had been a law clerk to the esteemed Justices Learned Hand and Felix Frankfurter. He had served Senator Leverett Saltonstall and Governor Christian Herter and had been an assistant in the Eisenhower administration. Moreover, Elliot Richardson, as U. S. Attorney for Massachusetts, had earned his own reputation as a foe of political corruption. From the party's viewpoint, Richardson was unbeatable.

The local Republicans gently suggested to Brooke that he withdraw. Brooke, just as gently, refused to budge. The powers then went to work on Brooke in earnest. First they offered him a judgeship. He declined it. They offered him their backing for the ceremonial post of Lieutenant Governor and he declined that. Finally a party spokesman took him aside and put it bluntly:

"Let's face it, Ed. Everybody who's anybody in the party is against you. You can't possibly win an election. You've already been defeated three times. You have none of the assets and *all* of the liabilities. You're a Republican in a Democratic state, a Protestant in a Catholic state, and a colored man in a Caucasian state—and besides, you're poor."

Brooke, refusing to accept these advance warnings of defeat, went out on what proved to be a successful search for delegates. By the time of the Republican nominating convention held in Worcester on June 17, 1962, he was certain of victory. What happened there provided one of the most unexpected thrillers in Massachusetts political history.

Following a number of personal accusations against each candidate by the opposing sides, the vote was taken. Richardson had 854 to Brooke's 845, and the Richardson forces went wild with joy. Many rushed immediately out of the hall to celebrate. Those left behind, including Brooke and his supporters, were stunned by a sudden an unexpected announcement made by Convention Chairman Saltonstall. The Richardson total, he declared, lacked *one vote* of being the necessary majority.

There followed a heated argument, some of it centering upon what should be done with the nine votes of a woman candidate who had dropped out of the race. Richardson's supporters sought to claim those votes but Saltonstall ordered a second ballot. The excited Brooke supporters shouted orders to their delegates. "Get back, get back—it isn't over yet," they cried. To those of his delegates not immediately in the hall, Brooke appealed by radio, urging their swift return. Those departed Richardson supporters were by then too immersed in their celebrators' revelry to be found. Among those who remained were several who had been pressured for one reason or another to vote for Richardson. But in this unexpected voting they switched votes, giving Brooke a 792 to 673 victory on the second ballot.

With this important primary victory, Brooke proceeded to use every asset to win the election. And it must be said that he is well endowed with assets. He has poise, good looks, and a soft musical voice. He dresses immaculately, and has been the most eloquent candidate produced in some time by either party. But could he, a Republican who happened also to be black, get a majority vote from a *white* electorate? That remained to be seen.

The Democrats had selected Frankie "Sweepstakes" Kelly as Brooke's election opponent. Mr. Kelly had at one time been Lieutenant Governor and Attorney General, and though he was popular in Boston's poorer sections, Bostonians at large regarded him as an old-line "machine" politician. The following episode during the campaign served as a distasteful reminder to staid Bostonians of the crude tactics of old-line machine politicos.

A gang of rough-looking, loud-talking blacks appeared mysteriously in the dignified residential sections of Wellesley and West Roxbury, in dented jalopies bearing Brooke stickers. The shabby unwelcome visitors, freely sipping "refreshments" from containers ill-concealed in paper bags, made loud inquiries about real estate. Before leaving they made known their intentions to "move in" as soon as Ed Brooke was elected Attorney General. No one of course, least of all the Kelly forces, claimed any knowledge of those colorful and, most likely, underpaid performers.

But if the skit was designed to injure Brooke's chances among middle- and upper-class whites, it failed completely. Indeed, it was that class who contributed heavily to Brooke's campaign. And when the votes were counted their man was ahead with a 260,000 plurality. In view of the racism revealed by the campaign there was doubtless much truth in the statement by one Democrat that the vote was not so much for Brooke as it was against Kelly. Attorney General Brooke dove into his new work with his customary zeal. Taking his campaign promises seriously, he sought to earnestly carry them through. Because he is an excellent lawyer who pays attention to legal details he surrounded himself with a first-rate staff. The latter were selected first on their merits rather than merely because they represented payment of his political debts.

The new Attorney General appealed to the public to co-operate with his office in exposing wrongdoing. Almost immediately be began to receive information, and public officials who had been cheating and stealing from the state were uncovered and indicted. One of them, a judge, had embezzled more than three quarters of a million dollars from public funds during the building of the Boston Common underground garage.

But Attorney General Brooke was not always cast in the role of Sir Galahad. He had to render tough decisions, many of them unpopular with many people. Moreover, he made errors. One particularly difficult decision involved him in a hassle with Boston's N.A.A.C.P. and other black civil rights groups. The latter, seeking an end to Boston's de facto school segregation, planned and staged a noisy 1963 sit-in demonstration at the Boston School Committee headquarters. They followed that by two boycotts in which thousands of black children stayed away from school. These actions naturally drew criticism from large areas of the city's white population, giving political strength to Mrs. Louise Day Hicks.

Mrs. Hicks, Chairman of the School Committee, was a shrill opponent of the local N.A.A.C.P.'s campaign. She had been, therefore, overwhelmingly returned to her Chairmanship by an irate white majority. And the Commissioner of Education promptly demanded of Attorney General Brooke that he rule on the legality of the boycott action taken by the N.A.A.C.P. Brooke, unable legally to prevent the boycotts, declared that parents participating in them *could* be fined up to $50 for each absent pupil. He then urged the N.A.A.C.P. leaders to call off both boycotts. But the latter, angered by both the segregated schools and Brooke's public position, would not budge. When they staged their boycotts the Attorney General was out of town.

Whites accused him of running from the issues. Blacks, recalling also that the Attorney General had left Roxbury and bought a home in the fashionable suburb of Newton, accused him of deserting *them.* Meanwhile, on an entirely different front, Brooke had angered both the schools and the churches by declaring that Massachusetts must adhere to the ruling of the U. S. Supreme Court against prayers in the public classroom. Public figures, Brooke was learning, are the constant targets from all angles.

The classical Brooke error with its ludicrously comic aspects, happens to have been based in a tragic series of nationally publicized murders. Along with his attacks on governmental corruption, the Attorney General took an active interest in trying to capture the "Boston Strangler." Over a period of two years, eleven Massachusetts women had been raped and choked to death by a presumed lone male assailant. Police work had failed to find their attacker.

During the stalemate Mr. Brooke's Assistant Attorney General and advisor John Bottomley came up with an extraordinary idea. Why not, he suggested, call in Peter Hurkos? They did. Hurkos, a man of Dutch birth living in California, was said to possess rare extrasensory perception. All other efforts having failed, Brooke reasoned that "we have everything to gain and nothing to lose." Besides, a group of private citizens had volunteered to pay Hurkos' fee.

The mystic arrived in Boston and, after viewing and touching items associated with the grisly crimes, began verbally to reconstruct the details of each case. Without hesitation he described the widely sought criminal as "a slight man with a sharp nose, a scar on his left arm, and a deformed thumb." With this detailed information the police fanned out to get their man.

They brought in not one but *two* shoe salesmen who fitted the description perfectly but who could not possibly be linked to the crimes. Then came the crowning irony. On his way home from Boston, Hurkos was himself seized by the F.B.I. and charged with having earlier passed himself off as an F.B.I. agent in Wisconsin. The Attorney General's political foes could barely contain their pleasure as they accused him of trying to resurrect the practice of witchcraft.

Brooke, nevertheless, decided to run for a second term as Attorney General in 1964. Disassociating himself from the hard line conservatism of Barry Goldwater, he presented himself simply to Bay State voters as Ed Brooke who wanted their support. In the national rout of Republicans led by Lyndon Johnson's victory over Goldwater, Brooke again won with an 800,000 majority. His was the largest plurality of any Republican in the nation. Now he was deserving of all the attention the national press showered upon him.

Many of the reporters revealed a belief that their readers were interested in the Massachusetts Attorney General not because of his proved abilities, but because he was black. And no matter how often Brooke hinted that he preferred to be viewed as a man in politics who happened to be black, interviewers invariably saw him and wrote of him as "that charming Negro in Massachusetts." And while many whites were lionizing Brooke as their number one spokesman for America's twenty million black people, he did manage to get across the idea that he had notions of moving higher up the political ladder.

Senator Leverett Saltonstall was seventy-three and several younger politicians, including Edward Brooke, felt that he should be thinking about retiring. Governor John Volpe had the same thought. Now, both he and Brooke were eyeing the Senate seat, though neither would say so publicly. The Attorney General was the first to break the silence. In a September 1965 press conference he matter-of-factly said he would run for the Senate if Saltonstall should decide not to. Governor Volpe was then forced to make his bid and Brooke promptly made a proposal to Volpe. Brooke would not stand in Volpe's way at all. If Volpe wanted the Senate seat he, Brooke, would gladly settle for the Governor's vacated seat.

Volpe gulped hard. He knew there was enough anti-black sentiment in Massachusetts to make Brooke unwanted as the state's number one figure. He thought again and he clearly recalled that Brooke's suave manner and his record at the polls *could* pull white votes. Suddenly John Volpe no longer wanted to leave the Governor's mansion for Mr. Saltonstall's seat in Washington.

Meanwhile, as pressures continued to urge his retirement, Senator Saltonstall announced at the end of 1965 that he was stepping down. Brooke immediately gathered up his wife and two daughters and took them to the Sheraton-Plaza Hotel, where they and his closest admirers saw and heard him say he would run for the Senate.

For fully a year Attorney General Brooke had been publicly, and constructively, critical of the Republican Party. At the beginning of 1965 he gave an interview to *U.S. News & World Report* in which he severely took his party to task. He revealed why he felt the Republicans had so little appeal to the average black voter. Pointing out that most Republican candidates fail to understand minority group needs and desires for equality in civil rights, he suggested two things. The first was a thorough study of their needs, and second was a new program designed to meet those needs.

Then in March of 1966 Little, Brown and Company, a Boston book publisher, brought out Brooke's *The Challenge of Change*. The book, an extension of Brooke's criticism of conservative Republicanism, really shook up the old guard. In it Brooke called for a foreign policy as mindful of the misery of underdeveloped peoples as it is of the "Communist conspiracy." He suggested greater investment in education as a deterrent to later investment in the dole. And he advised sweeping changes in the income tax structure—changes that would benefit the poor.

Such "radical" expression from a Republican political candidate would seem to sign his political death warrant as far as the conservatives at the primary were concerned. Still, convention delegates voted seven to one for Brooke's nomination. And things looked promising for him in the coming election until black unrest during the summer of 1966 took over the headlines. Brooke, aware of how latent white guilt and fear could hurt him under such circumstances, seized upon every opportunity to strengthen his position.

When Stokely Carmichael came to Boston, Brooke declared that the civil rights movement was going in the wrong direction. Roundly scoring Carmichael's oratory he said, "The term 'black power' is an unfortunate one. It acts like a spark and ignites the frustrations and tensions that are in the ghetto, and then you have riots."

Critics both black and white who felt Brooke was deliberately ignoring his own personal bouts with racism, in order to win an election controlled by white votes, were incensed by his stand. Brushing aside their remarks, Brooke proceeded with the business of his politics. The betting had placed him well ahead of his Democratic opponent, former Governor Endicott Peabody. And when on election day Brooke polled 62 per cent of the nearly two million votes cast many Americans were quite willing to believe that bigotry and white backlash had been decently buried in Massachusetts.

The new Senator's reception in Washington among his colleagues, particularly those from the south, was indeed friendly and cordial. Senator Ernest F. Hollings of South Carolina declared, "Senator Brooke owes his election to the white people of Massachusetts and I owe mine to the black people of South Carolina."

While rumblings of doubt of Brooke's identification with black men's problems vibrated and revibrated in the nation's black communities, there also were expressions of understanding from black leadership. Said Floyd McKissick:

"The black community has its fingers crossed on Brooke. If one is a politician in a white state, one relies on white votes. Right? Ed Brooke is one helluva politician. He has the appearance, the education, the intelligence; he has the middle-class standards white people like. If he's going to stay in politics, he'd better stay just what he's been."

Bayard Rustin, comparing Brooke with Congressman Adam Clayton Powell, said simply: "If you compare Brooke and Adam Powell on civil rights you cannot immediately give the edge to Powell."

Ebony Magazine, known for its Democratic leanings, did a story favorable to Brooke in its April 1967 issue. Writer Simeon Booker, taking the title for his article, "I'm a Soul Brother," directly from a Brooke quotation, gave the newly elected Senator a brotherly sendoff.

White America seemed comforted by Brooke's presence in the U. S. Senate. Even as he represented to them what the model black American should be, he also represented what they like to believe is their triumph over their own racial prejudices. Black America too was proud of Brooke—in spite of misgivings many blacks entertained of his interest in the welfare of the group. His severest black critics hoped that whenever the racial chips were down, Brooke would assert himself as a black American protesting bigotry. They did not have to wait too long to find out. With the election to the Presidency of Richard M. Nixon, the majority of black voters who had not supported him sucked in their breaths and watched.

Would the new Republican administration adhere to its campaign promise to end the war in Vietnam? Would it follow the recommendations Brooke set forth in *The Challenge of Change?* Would it be liberal and forward-looking in its view of minorities and the poor? Would it, in Mr. Nixon's own words, "bring us together"? These were the things that Brooke and other liberal Republicans who worked for Mr. Nixon's election hoped the President would seek to do. They were the things that black voters at large never expected of the new President in the first place.

Within a year President Nixon nominated South Carolina's Clement F. Haynsworth, judge of the U. S. Fourth Circuit Court of Appeals, to the U. S. Supreme Court vacancy created by the departure of Abe Fortas. The nation's labor and civil rights groups, recalling Judge Haynsworth's past rulings that were not favorable to either labor or black Americans, lobbied against the Haynsworth confirmation.

Senator Brooke cast his vote against confirmation and Judge Haynsworth did not become a member of the U. S. Supreme Court.

A second appointment by Mr. Nixon, Judge G. Harrold Carswell, another southerner, likewise stirred restlessness among supporters of civil rights. Senator Brooke carefully reviewed the record as a judge of Carswell, who had in his private life supported white supremacy precepts. Again Brooke joined those voting against Carswell's confirmation and Mr. Nixon had to look about for a more acceptable nominee. Black Americans smiled knowingly. Ed Brooke knew who he was, all right.

In commenting on the Nixon record after the first eighteen months, Senator Brooke said: "President Nixon said he wanted to bring us together, but everything he has done so far appears to be desgined to push us further apart."

When Mr. Nixon announced the deployment of American troops to Cambodia, Brooke declared that "the President has undertaken an extremely hazardous policy." Such statements from a hard-core "radical" would, in the national conservative climate, be easily discounted. But Edward W. Brooke is no radical. He is a brilliant and a successful lawyer who has learned how to survive and how to advance in one of the biggest—and toughest—political arenas in the world.

But there is still one other thing about him worth remembering. His ability to get there, and more importantly to stay there with dignity, is due to the lessons he has learned as a black American. When in that *Ebony* interview with Simeon Booker he laughingly said, "You can say that I am a soul brother," he knew profoundly just what he was talking about.

Kenneth Bancroft Clark

HE IS A slightly built, mild-mannered, soft-spoken man. Few people seeing him casually for the first time would ever suspect that he is one of the nation's eminent psychologists and authors. Though he has been labeled a "moderate," the label hardly fits Dr. Kenneth B. Clark, for if ever there was a vigorous and devastating critic of government administrations that ignore and neglect the needs of impoverished Americans, he is it. Moreover, when he speaks of impoverished persons he is talking as much about the uninformed as he is about the ill-fed, ill-clothed, and ill-housed.

Dr. Clark is known and respected by virtually all black leaders, including those who have differed with him. As has been mentioned earlier, he worked closely with the N.A.A.C.P. when Supreme Court Justice Thurgood Marshall was chief of its legal staff. He also worked with Martin and Coretta King during the Montgomery, Alabama, bus boycott. Dr. Clark thoroughly understood the anger of Malcolm X. Though he did not agree with all of Malcolm's recommendations he respected Malcolm's intelligence and integrity. Along with many others he was profoundly shaken by Malcolm's violent death.

Floyd McKissick, Bayard Rustin, Whitney Young, Roy Wilkins, and at least four U. S. Presidents are but a sampling of those who admire and respect the knowledge and judgment of this remarkable social scientist. In his field he ranks very high.

Arthur Bancroft Clark was an inspector for the United Fruit Company in the Canal Zone in Panama, where his son was born on July 24, 1914. It was agreed that the infant boy would be named Kenneth and both parents, especially his mother, Miriam, had great hopes for him. Indeed, Miriam Clark found the easygoing ways of the humid Central American environment not at all in keeping with her ambitions for their two children. She tried to get her husband to leave and return to the United States, where, she believed, opportunities were more numerous. Arthur refused, so Miriam bundled little Kenneth and his two-year-old sister and brought them on to New York, where they settled in Central Harlem.

Miriam had taught Kenneth to read even before he was enrolled in school so that when it was time for him to enter P.S. 139 he was quite able to handle the reading. The same was not true of many of his schoolmates who also were products of broken homes. But Kenneth did long to be like them in one respect. In true boyish fashion he greatly admired the athletic skills of his husky classmates. How he wished he could have competed with them as they ran and jumped and played ball with such strength and agility. But such was not for him and he knew it. Kenneth was one of the smallest boys in his class, so rather than risk physical injury by indulging in rough-and-tumble play he sought other outlets for his energies. He found one of these outlets at the corner of Lenox Avenue and 135th Street, in the exciting world in the New York Public Library. Soon he became a regular visitor and a regular borrower.

One day as he browsed about in the children's section he decided to take a chance on climbing the stairs to the top floor. Kenneth had never before ventured up there, for that section was reserved, or so it seemed, for adults and he was only twelve. As he reached the top of the stairs and turned into the open door a slightly rotund, well-dressed man with brown skin and curly black hair rose from the desk and walked over to him. The man greeted Kenneth pleasantly as he curled an arm around his shoulder, led him to a reading table, and sat down to talk with him. Not once did he ask the boy what he was looking for upstairs. He assumed that Kenneth was interested in books and in what he could learn from them. That is the kind of man Arthur Schomburg was. He too had been curious about books when he was Kenneth's age.

When Schomburg was a boy in his native Puerto Rico, he asked his teacher one day why there were no stories of black people of worth in his school books. When the teacher replied that black people had done little or nothing worthy of mention in books, little Arthur Schomburg was hurt and dismayed. He could not bring himself to believe what his teacher had said. So he decided that when he became old enough he would search for books that contained stories of the achievements of black people. He did just that and his search was a successful one. It was so successful that he acquired a collection too large to manage alone. Happily he was able to get the New York Public Library to purchase and house the material and to place him in charge of what is known today as the Schomburg Collection of the New York Public Library.

So young Kenneth Clark's quiet and voluntary visit to the upstairs room that was then the Schomburg Collection touched a sensitive response in the older man. It also revealed a new world to the boy, who years later wrote an account of that meeting with Arthur Schomburg:

"We talked about books. We talked about wonderful things: about the history of human beings, about the contributions of Negroes which were to be found in books . . .

"On that first day of meeting Schomburg, I knew I had met a friend. He did not ask me if I had come from a broken home. He didn't ask me whether my mother was poor. He never told me to improve myself. He merely looked and saw that I was a human being who was probably desperately hungry more for human acceptance than even for the nourishment which could be found in books. He accepted me as a human being and through this acceptance helped me to share his love of, and his excitement in the world of books."

As Kenneth Clark began to know the books in the Schomburg Collection he learned how books can be used to justify man's wrongdoing. He found, for instance, a book written by a man in the Christian ministry who declared that the beast of the field was the Negro. And the author's name carried behind it a string of degrees! So as young Clark continued to read and to study he resolved that he would have to devote his life to the pursuit of as much balanced truth as he could find. And should he ever write and have his writings published they would have to be as honest and as factual as he could possibly make them.

When it came time for Kenneth to enter high school his mother brooked no nonsense whatever with New York school authorities. For many years it was the custom for white teachers of black children in northern urban schools automatically to shunt those children off to high schools specializing in vocational training. Just as Malcolm X had been advised by a teacher that law was not "a realistic career for a nigger to pursue," so it was that a teacher advised Kenneth Clark to enter one of New York's vocational high schools. Miriam Clark was enraged.

Rushing off to see the teacher who gave her son such advice, she even embarrassed Kenneth by forcefully declaring that he would enter a vocational school only over her dead body. The following autumn Kenneth was enrolled at the academically oriented George Washington High School, where his record prepared him later to enter Howard University. There, majoring in psychology, he received his B.A. degree in 1935 and his M.A. the following year. Recalling his course in political science taught by Dr. Ralph J. Bunche, Clark has warm reminiscences of that period of his development:

"There were men at Howard who in the thirties were as clear about racial injustice as everyone believes people are now. Those guys made the issues very clear."

In his senior year at Howard, Kenneth Clark met pretty Mamie Phipps, daughter of an Arkansas physician and freshman math major. He persuaded her to switch her major to psychology and, during the following year, to become a member of the class he was teaching. Meanwhile the two began to "go steady." Mamie Phipps was as intelligent as she was good-looking.

"I was hoping she would get a B in my course but I had to give her an A," Kenneth later admitted. "She was a very excellent student."

The couple married in 1938 as Mamie took her bachelor's degree and *magna cum laude* honors. Her mother's fears that marriage might bring an end to the young bride's studies disappeared as Mamie Clark quickly took her master's degree at Howard. Then she and Kenneth went to New York to work for their doctorates at Columbia University. Kate, the first of their two children, was born in 1940. Kenneth, meanwhile, had taught briefly at Howard University, Hampton Institute, and New York City's Queens College.

It was 1942 when he joined the faculty of New York's

City College, where he was later to become its first permanent black professor. The country was at war and there were charges that, because of discrimination in the armed forces as well as in the nation's war-oriented industries, morale among black Americans was running low. The Office of War Information quickly looked about for a trained observer to travel about the country to investigate the allegations. They chose Kenneth Clark.

For about a year Dr. Clark performed that service in his thorough-going and highly professional way. His scholarship drew the attention of Swedish social scientist Gunnar Myrdal, who added Clark to his staff of researchers. Myrdal was preparing his famed two-volume study, *An American Dilemma,* and he needed Kenneth Clark's talents in the area of psychology. These early assignments marked the beginning of a number of scientific studies that Clark was to make in the interest of exposing injustice based upon race discrimination.

But Kenneth Clark, the social scientist, is opposed to any kind of human injustice, especially if it is directed at children. In 1946 he and Mamie founded the Northside Center for Child Development. The Center, operating on the slogan "The mental health program in Harlem must expand," initially functioned for black children alone. But in 1949, when it moved to its present West 110th Street location, it became interracial. With the aid of foundation grants the Northside Center began its function as a diagnostic and treatment center for emotionally disturbed children. Its staff of psychiatrists, psychologists, and psychiatric social workers launched its work with children from broken homes, whose feeling of rejection resulted in their resentment and confusion. As Clark explained it to a reporter during a 1949 interview, "A child who comes here is not a file or number, but a personality. We do everything we can within our limits."

Dr. Mamie Clark directed the Northside Center and her husband served as Assistant Director. Their view that work with confused adults was just as necessary as work with children was borne out by Kenneth's talks with adult groups. Addressing a New York City panel in 1952 he warned that many well-intentioned parents may engender prejudice in their children by teaching them to "keep up with the Joneses" and to "pursue the gods of success and status." Many parents, it seems, believe that is the way children learn to deal with life's realities.

Not so, said Dr. Clark. He then suggested that parents should teach children instead to use their intellects critically in dealing with the realities of life. He further suggested that parents instill in their children some basic moral standards for use in the home, so that their children will have a gauge by which they can properly measure social situations outside the home. That suggestion was given support by another panelist, a minister of East Harlem's First Spanish Evangelical Church, who observed that children are direct reflections of their parents' attitudes.

But Kenneth Clark was not satisfied merely to address himself and his beliefs to local audiences in New York City. He wrote a book for parents titled simply *Prejudice and Your Child*. It was a small book published in 1955 by the Beacon Press in Boston, but its clear and honest writing transformed the slender work into a giant among studies of its type. Critical praise for *Prejudice and Your Child* was unstinting.

The Library Journal had the following to say of it: "A probing, thoroughgoing consideration of a pressing problem in America today, this book should be read by all adults included in the various groups mentioned (schools, churches, social agencies, parents)."

The New York Times called it "practical and factual (and went on to say that) this book tells how and when children get their prejudices, what it does to a child's growing personality to be discriminated against (and) how prejudice hurts a 'majority group' child."

The name of social scientist Kenneth Bancroft Clark, was becoming known to a nationwide audience and he was just past forty years old.

Then, as has been previously said, Thurgood Marshall called Clark into a case he had before the U. S. Supreme Court. Marshall, then with the N.A.A.C.P., had set his legal sights on southern school segregation and he needed Clark's scientific testimony to help him win. Following that victory Dr. Clark delivered a speech in Boston in May of 1956. The occasion was the annual dinner of the Unitarian Service Committee Inc. and newspaper coverage of the event indicated in optimistic headlines that Dr. Clark had predicted the end of southern school segregation by 1961.

Careful examination of the Clark remarks, however, revealed the studied caution of the social scientist. What Dr. Clark actually said was that "if desegregation does not occur within five years the South and the nation will have retrogressed . . . I do not believe that Americans will permit this to happen."

As a reminder to the forgetful, Kenneth Clark cited a few of the blocks standing in the way of school desegregation. Among them were the stubbornness of segregated patterns, the apathy of those not immediately concerned, and the seesawing on the issue by politicians and the legislative and executive branches of the Federal government.

The five-year period that Dr. Clark allotted for either the desegregation of southern schools or the "retrogression" of the nation was over. At a New York meeting of psychologists an obviously disappointed Kenneth Clark declared that the acuteness of racial violence indicated that the nation might be in a state of "terminal dry rot." While attributing violent black uprisings to violent white determination to keep black Americans subservient, he saw the nation caught in the fire of violence induced and fed by the war in Vietnam. Alluding to the violence committed by the United States troops against Vietnam civilians, he noted: "I saw all too clearly the relationship between the violence in Vietnam and in our cities."

Vietnam, he declared, had made blacks and whites so "inured to violence" that Americans see violence as the answer to their problems. The black American, he found, had reasoned that it is "better to die quickly in a society incapable of bringing about justice instead of stringing the suffering out for a lifetime." Kenneth Clark made it clear that he saw the black man's use of violence in retaliation against white oppression as the signal for his own destruction. He could see it no other way as he recognized the grim accuracy of Martin Luther King, Jr.'s despairing description of America as "the greatest purveyor of violence on earth." He also shared King's and Floyd McKissick's view of our sporadic racial disorders as related to our nation's organized violence in Vietnam.

But Dr. Clark saw something even more threatening to America as he concluded his address to that body of psychologists and psychiatrists at New York's Roosevelt Hotel. Whites, he told them, are seeking to maintain their superior status by greater violence against blacks. But the tragic fallacy in this is that "you cannot have superior status if all the people over whom you were superior are dead."

The N.A.A.C.P. in 1961 presented its coveted Spingarn Medal to Kenneth Clark. The award, an annual citation, goes to that black individual who, in the opinion of the organization, has done most to advance race relations. In making the award the N.A.A.C.P. noted that as Dr. Clark went about his work he was consistently in advance of the

nation at large. How right they were about Kenneth
Clark. He had barely received the Spingarn Medal than he
assumed yet another advance position.

The fight of the black American, he asserted, is not for
himself alone. It is up to the black American, in Dr.
Clark's view, to help America regain its soul.

"The basic issue is whether we have democracy in this
country—or we don't have it," he said in a 1961 interview.
"There's no sense talking any more. We've argued the
argument out. No amount of hypocritical double-talk is
going to save us. The issue isn't the right of Negroes to
ride buses without insult or to be served in restaurants
with clean spoons. We've gone way beyond self pity or
protest. The issue is very simple: No American can have
his rights abrogated in any part of America.

"I can't understand how we expect to be taken seriously
about a free Berlin when we're absolutely confused about
Jackson, Mississippi. What's so much more precious about
Berlin than Jackson or Birmingham or Atlanta? . . . The
sooner America gets out of he old-fashioned notion that
desegregation means Negroes pushing for rights at the expense of white people, the better it will be for our country. The Negro, in demanding his rights unqualified and
uncompromised, is contributing to the strength of America in the perilous days ahead. I like to think this democracy has that strength."

It would have been impossible for Kenneth Clark to
have been reared in Harlem and to have established a
treatment clinic without knowing northern racism for
what it is. He knew that many southern states were using
local laws along with the power of local police and politicians to deny black southerners their rights. He knew
that when black migrants went north they were fleeing the
visible and flagrant signs of discrimination. They were
fleeing outright and undisguised segregation in places of

public accommodation. Once in the north they found another kind of discrimination—one more subtle and capricious. And it was found most consistently in employment, in housing, and in schools.

Reasoning that he could more effectively fight such injustice from an inside position, he made a move in that direction. In 1962 he founded and became staff director of HARYOU, Harlem Youth Opportunities Unlimited, Inc. He also became chairman of HARYOU's Board of Directors even as he continued to hold his professorship at New York's City College. The program, one of several inaugurated by President Lyndon B. Johnson, was described to the people of Harlem, the nation's largest ghetto, as the nation's war on poverty.

As a social scientist, Dr. Clark was proud of the 118-million-dollar project. In planning it he had prepared a superb 614-page report on conditions of poverty in Harlem. He titled his document *Youth in the Ghetto*. Not only does the report contain indisputable information on Harlem but it also contains a program to cure that community's many ills. Among other things, it calls for the establishment of forty preschool centers where black children can be prepared for education. There are plans also for rehabilitating children involved with the police. And there are plans for art and culture centers. As Clark envisioned it HARYOU's self-help program would have been the largest of its sort in the nation. Yes, Kenneth Clark was justly proud and pleased. But neither his pride nor pleasure were to be sustained.

Local politicians, sparked by Harlem Congressman Adam Powell, wanted to control HARYOU. Their desire to control it was supported by Harlemites who did not understand why such a program should be kept out of politics if it were to be truly beneficial to the community. And Clark, possessing none of Congressman Powell's popularity or charisma as far as Harlem citizens were concerned, received little community support for his program. Though he told the people of Harlem that Powell had threatened to use his Congressional chairmanship to withhold Federal money from HARYOU, Clark was pushed out of the program he created. An aide of Powell headed the project, which bore little resemblance to and had little of the character of the one Dr. Clark had originally conceived and presented.

But out of the ashes of Kenneth Clark's defeat by petty district politics, he was able to erect another creation of *national* import. Using the 614-page HARYOU plan titled *Youth in the Ghetto* as a guide, he wrote *Dark Ghetto,* which was published in May 1965 by Harper and Row. The book, carefully documented and written not as a polemic but as an incisive analysis of life in central Harlem, received splendid reviews.

Its chapter titled "Getto Schools: Separate and Unequal" was particularly applicable to the acutely painful New York City school condition at the time of its publication. New York City residents were in a hassle with each other over their schools. Three civil rights school boycotts, led by Brooklyn's black Presbyterian minister, the Reverend Milton A. Galamison, and two white boycotts had already interrupted the routine of the 1965 school year. A school superintendent had been ousted in a disturbingly deceptive way, and black and white parents grew alternately frustrated and angry with public officials and with one another. To make matters worse, the United Federation of Teachers was threatening a strike for the following September.

Against such a turbulent background the authoritative study with its recommendations for improving the situation merited the honors that came to Dr. Clark. He was given the Kurt Lewin Memorial Award of the Society for the Psychological Study of Social Issues. That highest honor in the field of social psychology is awarded each year for "outstanding contributions to the development and integration of psychological research and social action."

Early in 1966 Dr. Clark was elected to the policy-making New York State Board of Regents. His was the first designation of a black man to that fifteen-member body in the Board's 182 years, and it was greeted with elation by those seeking to end racial imbalance in New York's schools. One expression of approval came from *The New York Post*. On February 10, 1966, it commented editorially in the following way:

"The cause of educational excellence in New York has received a big boost in recent days.

"The State Legislature's election of Prof. Kenneth Clark to the Board of Regents adds to that body a public-spirited scholar endowed with originality of thought and a capacity to do battle on behalf of conclusions that reflective inquiry supports.

"While many scholars turn library and laboratory into a refuge from the stormy problems of contemporary life, Prof. Clark uses them as fortresses from which to deal powerful blows on behalf of equality and justice.

"The Board of Regents is fortunate to acquire as a member someone who has thought so deeply about how to make our educational system more responsive to the needs of Negro and Puerto Rican youngsters."

Kenneth Clark, while pleased that such an honor had come to him, was cautiously realistic.

"I can't see," he remarked, "how you can realistically expect one member of the board to end de facto segregation. It can't be done by magic."

He went on to explain that the problems of the school system are too complex to be solved simply by abolishing neighborhood schools. And he recognized that teacher shortages, overcrowding, and plant shortages plus official bureaucracy also complicate racial strife.

Even with such misgivings, Dr. Clark did not shy away from the obligations of his new assignment. In October 1966, charging that pupils in New York's ghetto schools were receiving a "criminally inferior education," he further accused the city school board of "inaction, indifference, apathy, and insensitivity." Encouraged by having just been honored along with his wife by Columbia University for their "influential humanitarian work," he concluded his criticisms of the Board of Education with these words:

"I am now prepared to ask my colleagues on the Board of Regents and the Commissioner of the State of New York, Dr. James E. Allen, Jr., and his staff to make a thorough probing evaluation of the quality of education provided for Negro and white students in the public schools of New York City at this time."

Life for Kenneth Clark, member of the Board of Regents, became busier and more complex. In addition to his new work with the State Board, he was still holding a professorship at City College and codirecting the Northside Center with his wife. Moreover, he had found the time and the energy to co-edit with Talcott Parsons *The Negro American,* published by Houghton Mifflin in 1966. He was submerged in work and something had to be dropped. So in the interest of preserving both his health and his tradition of professional performance, he gave up the Assistant Directorship of the Northside Center.

This was by no means a signal that he was abandoning or forgetting youth. Indeed, he had had a teenage daughter and son just a few years earlier. And because he was especially attuned to what was happening to the nation's black youth he wrote an article about them for *Ebony*

Magazine's August 1967 issue. The essay was titled "The Search for Identity" and it was obviously intended to inform and reassure adult readers so frequently confused by young people's actions.

Dr. Clark began by reminding readers that the civil rights movement during the 1950s was led by a *young* Martin Luther King, Jr., still in his mid-twenties. It also mentioned the daring and the courage of young members of the Student Nonviolent Coordinating Committee and similarly motivated groups as they challenged southern customs. Those student groups, he pointed out, sought their identity through unlimited absorption into the American mainstream.

Clark then reviewed the separatist followers of Malcolm X with their "natural" hairdos and African-inspired dress. These youths, mainly of the black lower economic level, seek self-esteem by separating themselves as completely as is humanly possible from the white American mainstream. Nor are they alone, declares the psychologist. Many young middle-class black college students insist upon living as closely together as possible while they attend predominantly white universities and colleges. This, in contrast to what Clark calls the "anonymous, wishful, protective denial of their race" practiced by black students of the past, is yet another search for identity.

Even young black rioters, he declares, seek self-esteem: "This is the way those who have absolutely nothing to lose seek a pathetic affirmation of self, even if it is obtained moments before death."

Dr. Clark is quick to admit that this search for identity is heavily involved in turmoil. But he accepts turmoil as a part of the process of growth and transition.

"No human beings," he says, "can move from being the victim of extremes of injustice and inhumanity to the goals

of self-acceptance and positive and personal and racial
identity without it."

But if Dr. Clark sees black turmoil as an evil to be expected, he also sees the effects of racism on whites, especially white youth. Speaking before a Senate hearing in
Washington, D.C., on April 20, 1970, he pointed out how
segregation is inciting sensitive white youngsters to self-
destructive acts of rebellion. School segregation, he explained, cannot be properly dealt with on a purely political basis. It becomes an issue at once moral, ethical, and
educational.

Young white people, noting the nation's inconsistency
in talking democratic values while perpetuating undemo-
cratic practices in education, are in rebellion. They are
showing, Dr. Clark declared, their distaste for the patterns
of hypocrisy practiced by their society. And he told Senator Jacob K. Javits of New York that "educationally" it
was "imperative" for whites to have exposure to blacks in
the classroom and vice versa. And Dr. Clark concluded,
"The increasing instability in white youth tells us we have
waited too long."

It is such clear and forthright thinking that has earned
Dr. Clark numerous awards, honorary degrees, and the
respect of the world's community of social scientists. And
if you have the feeling that with all the professional ac-
claim and the honors that he has never lost touch with
the dark ghetto of his youth, you are completely right. It
is doubtful that he ever will.

Ruby Dee

RUBY DEE RELAXES on the sun porch of her comfortable suburban home sipping parsley tea and talking easily. At one point her voice grows quiet and somber.

"All that morning," she murmurs, "I had been singing. And I am not a singer and I don't really know this song. But I sang the words over and over . . .

> Another man done gone,
> Another man done gone!

And then this terrible depression overtook me. A little later that day we had word that Malcolm had been shot to death."

The Malcolm to whom Ruby alluded was, of course, Malcolm X.

She is a petite woman, beautifully proportioned and strongly put together. To call her "pretty" or "cute" is to miss the essence of her remarkable good looks. You look closely at her and you see a fully mature woman with a firm, youthful face and body. But what you remember about Ruby Dee—*really* remember about her—is that inner beauty of sensitive intelligence and awareness of the world about her. Those are the qualities in her that make what

she does as an artist so meaningful. They are the qualities
that reach out from the stage and the screen and touch
with such force those seeking the dignity of full manhood
and full womanhood.

She was christened Ruby Wallace and she was born in
Cleveland, Ohio. Her father, Edward Marshall Wallace,
a native of Tennessee, worked on the railroad. Her mother,
Emma A. Benson Wallace, a South Carolinian, had been
a teacher. While the four Wallace children, three girls and
a boy, were young, their parents moved to New York's
Harlem.

Harlem, during the period of Ruby's childhood, was
just beginning to deteriorate into the ghetto it now is. It
was still the favorite playground for downtown white
New Yorkers and out-of-town visitors seeking exciting
New York night life. White patrons with money to spend
packed the Cotton Club to hear Duke Ellington's famous
"jungle rhythms" and Cab Calloway's "hi-de-ho" band.
Even though stars like dancer Bill "Bojangles" Robinson
and singers Ethel Waters and Adelaide Hall drew hordes
of white fans to the Cotton Club, rarely were there black
patrons among them. It was the policy of the gangsters
who operated the night spot to keep its guest list as lily-
white as possible. It was some little time then before black
patrons of Harlem's Apollo Theatre were to see a pretty
young singer and dancer who had been a teen-age Cotton
Club chorus girl. Her name was Lena Horne.

Harlemites who wanted to "swing" in Harlem went to
Connie's Inn, the Renaissance Ballroom, and the black-
owned Savoy Ballroom. The latter place, known as "The
Homeland of Happy Feet," presented great black musical
aggregations. A feature of the Savoy was Chick Webb, a
hunchback drummer from Baltimore, who gave a shy
orphan girl singer named Ella Fitzgerald a chance to sing
and record with his band.

Along with the Harlem-based musicians and entertainers in Harlem there were the colorful sports figures who lived there. Aging Harry Wills, the original "Black Panther" of boxing, was one. Though Wills' handlers changed their great heavyweight's nickname to *"Brown* Panther" to make him appear less menacing to whites, they were never able to get their fighter a match with champion Jack Dempsey. Jet-black "Kid Chocolate"—a phenomenal Cuban featherweight with patent-leather processed hair—was another Harlemite whose likeness appeared regularly in *Ring* Magazine through the drawings of black artist Ted Carroll. There was the Renaissance Five, a basketball team, whose home court was the polished floor of the Renaissance Ballroom. "The Rennys" were thrilling black and white fans with their wizardry long before the Harlem Globetrotters came on the scene.

But if Harlem was a playground for whites and a gold mine for its few talented and fortunate blacks, it was something else for its average citizens. Those who didn't live in relative luxury on upper Edgecombe and St. Nicholas avenues, called "Sugar Hill," had to struggle for an existence. Most, like Ruby's parents, had come from the south seeking more lucrative work and better schooling for their children. And the times for them were hard.

Those lacking strong family ties drifted and fell prey to the assorted hustlers of whom Malcolm X was one before his conversion to The Nation of Islam. Others were delayed on the way to oblivion by a tall robed black man with a heavy mane of white hair, who walked the streets of Harlem barefoot warning all who would listen of their impending destruction. And there was also a squat black religious cult leader who called himself Father Divine, who fed a lot of hungry Harlemites unable to afford more than fifteen cents for a meal. Ruby's family, living in the very heart of Harlem, was a strong and close-knit unit.

"Though I grew up in what we call 'The Ghetto,' she recalls, "I did have people around me who cared. I was next to the youngest and they cushioned me from the deprivations to the point where I didn't even know I *was* deprived. It's the *not caring* that means 'Ghetto' to children today."

Elaborating upon this, Ruby speaks of the mothers of misbehaving schoolgirls who were sent for by the teachers and who came to the school to get the details of their children's wrongdoing. She remembers those sessions in which teachers discussed openly and in front of the class what had happened. And irate hard-working mothers proceeded then and there to punish the girls, with the promise that more would be forthcoming when the latter arrived home.

"I don't know the value of this, if any," she says. "But life was simpler then and most girls feared that kind of embarrassment enough to, at least, behave in the classroom."

Ruby describes her mother—who is really her stepmother and the only mother she ever knew—as an industrious woman with great managerial skills. Emma Amelia Wallace *had* to manage well. Her husband's earnings as a non-union railroad man consisted mainly of tips—often scant—and she not only fed her family but sewed for them as well. She found legitimate ways of earning extra money and she managed well enough to permit the children to have violin and piano lessons. To a woman who had been a teacher and who was a strict disciplinarian such things were important.

Her children were not permitted to run the streets and when she felt they needed fresh air she permitted them to sit on the fire escape. There the youngsters could see what was going on in the street below without becoming physically involved. And they saw plenty. One sight she will never forget was that of two black limousines roaring up the street as their occupants exchanged gunfire. Another was that of a boy tossed high in the air as a speeding car struck his bicycle. Such sights made her glad her parents were so strict with their children.

Mrs. Wallace had been an elocutionist, who had wanted so much, as a girl, to be in the theater. She had worked briefly with the great black actor Richard B. Harrison, who achieved fame late in life in the role of "De Lawd" in Marc Connelly's *Green Pastures*. Ruby would listen spellbound as her mother recited the poems of her favorite lyric writer, black Paul Lawrence Dunbar, who had died of tuberculosis at the age of thirty-four. One of her favorites was "In the Morning," a poem describing the shrill morning "getting up call" of a mother to her sleepyhead son.

In such a home atmosphere the Wallace children were given an appreciation of the value of learning. Ruby learned to sew and draw before she reached her teens, and at the same period she developed a love of poetry and the spoken arts. When company came each child was expected to perform in some way before he could be "excused," for, as Ruby Dee explains it, "our worth, it seems, was summed up in what we could offer of ourselves and of what we did in school." Since school assignments required outside reading the Wallace children were taught early that they must use the facilities of the New York Public Library. So Ruby went regularly to the branch at 135th Street and Lenox Avenue, the same one used by Kenneth Clark and James Baldwin. The thing was to *learn*. And one learned so that one could *amount* to something, so that he could eventually leave the tenements with their rats, roaches, and roomers.

Ruby attended Harlem's elementary P.S. 133 and from there she went on to Junior High School 136. Because she loved English and poetry she began to lean toward the arts, particularly the spoken arts. Some of her poetry was published in the New York *Amsterdam News,* a black weekly newspaper, and she earned her first money drawing maps and charts for nurses at Harlem Hospital. Nor was her zest for learning or accomplishing diminished when she left the comparative safety of P.S. 133 to enter notoriously wicked P.S. 136.

In speaking of the horrors of P.S. 136 Ruby says, "I was so motivated as to have missed all of that. It wasn't until after I had gotten out of P.S. 136 that I became fully aware of the prostitution, lesbianism, and the relationship of the girls to the police. How lucky I was to get through unscathed!"

Because black girls in Harlem were being "educated" to become domestics, because many in Harlem felt that the school system had such limited aspirations for them, Ruby wanted to get into a first-rate high school. Hunter High School, one of New York's best for girls, was her choice.

To get into Hunter one had to take a stiff test. Academic excellence was the prime requirement and girls from the black ghetto who made the grade had to be able, for Hunter attracted bright girls from all areas of New York City. Says Ruby Dee:

"The whole school became involved as we took those tests because it would be a feather in everybody's cap if students from our Harlem school would make it. We waited for days for the results of the tests to come back and when they did classes almost stopped. And when we learned that six or eight girls from our school had made it, believe me when I tell you that their achievement was cause for celebration!"

Ruby never forgot P.S. 136, and they never forgot her. In 1962 they invited her back to receive their Lady of the Year Award.

"I looked at this sea of black girls and their white teachers," she recalls, "and I saw the hunger in the children's faces. I knew in my soul they weren't getting the food they needed in order to be the whole human beings they had to be. And the saddest and the most exciting time was the reception those girls gave me—coming as I did from that school. I was never so moved in my life!"

Hunter High School girls generally go to college, and with four children in the Wallace family there was only one hope for Ruby if she wanted an education beyond high school. She would have to be a good student so that she could pass the competitive test for entry into tuition-free Hunter College. But one had first to get through high school, and Ruby found the transition from rough-and-ready Junior High School 136 in Harlem to Hunter High School a traumatic experience. The white girls at Hunter had come from more privileged environments. Their clothes were expensive and their collective manner, in contrast to that of Harlem girls, was of complete self-confidence and self-possession.

Though Ruby Wallace lacked the fine clothes of many of her Hunter High schoolmates, she did not lack self-confidence. Her mother had helped instill that in her as she taught her to recite and to carry herself with poise and dignity. Moreover, Ruby had learned to use her fists in the struggle for survival in grammar school. So she was prepared to make the adjustment to the new school environment, and though it was a hard task she was equal to it. She had unexpected help from the black music teacher, Miss Peace, who constantly encouraged her to go as far and as swiftly as she could.

With a strong mother at home and with Miss Peace in her corner at Hunter High, Ruby was able to cope with her first rebuff in the integrated high school. It occurred when she tried to get a part in a play. The teacher, a

woman who was generally pleasant and of whom Ruby was
genuinely fond, replied softly and in all seriousness to
Ruby's inquiry, "But, Ruby there aren't any *maid's* parts
in this play." That did it! Ruby Wallace never again tried
to be in a play or a drama at Hunter High. But she read
aloud at every opportunity. And she prepared for entry
into Hunter College. At one point her sensitive awareness of the unconscious air of superiority among her white
schoolmates began to affect her studies. She knew they
weren't deliberately *trying* to act superior—that they were
playing their unconscious role in the racist drama so terribly real in America. Still, the effects were the same and
she felt them. However, Ruby couldn't let her schoolmates' problems stop her. She made up her academic
deficiencies in summer school and went on to Hunter
College.

By now she had become accustomed to the manner of
her white fellow students. And she had developed an interest in the theater groups in Harlem. There was the
American Negro Theatre, which she joined shortly after
entering college. And the first play she appeared in was
On Striver's Row, a comedy about Harlem life. Abe Hill
was its director and when Ruby auditioned for the part
of the debutante, Hill said brusquely, "Speak louder
please." She got the part. Meanwhile, she continued with
her studies at Hunter, majoring in French and Spanish.

The American Negro Theatre had no money. Unlike
the Federal Theatre in Harlem, funded during the mid-
1930s by the U. S. Government, the A.N.T. had to make it
wholly on the dedication of its members. Unlike the Harlem Federal group it had no Orson Welles and John
Houseman to help them present such spectaculars as the
Federal Theatre's *Macbeth.* Abe Hill's little group sold its
own tickets, at depression prices, from door to door in
Harlem. Its own performers swept the floor of its theater

—an auditorium in the basement of the 135th Street Library—and they shoveled snow away from the doors so patrons could get in.

But help and inspiration came from without as well as from within. A director visiting from the Soviet Union gladly accepted an invitation to guest-direct a play. Osceola Archer taught speech. Three young actors who were later to become world-famous started there. They were Earl Hyman, Sidney Poitier, and Harry Belafonte.

"They made it a rich experience," Ruby Dee muses, "one that happened because it had to. I regard my work with The American Negro Theatre as the most memorable and important thing about my training. I do not insist it was at all like that at The Royal Academy in London, but it was the best we could get. Then came *Anna Lucasta,* a smash hit. Broadway syphoned off the best black actors in the group and there was division among us as Broadway success made us—ha!—a commodity!"

Not yet through Hunter College, Ruby affiliated herself with a class in radio training at the American Theatre Wing. There she met two men who helped her get into radio. One was Kenneth MacGregor, a man whose insights were deep enough to make him turn a deaf ear to the trigger-tempered Ruby who bawled him out for being late to class. Somewhere out of the depths of his human experience, MacGregor sensed what being black and rejected does to one's personality, and he was quickly forgiving.

The other man was Arthur Hannah.

"I was doing audition material for Arthur Hannah and I decided to try all kinds of ethnic material—the kinds of things I was sure white folks would like—maids—and dialect. And I'll never forget that Hannah said to me very gently, 'Ruby, you don't have to do that. Don't insult me by doing that. Let's hear you do some of the other material you have.''

Ruby Dee smiles as she recounts the story and concludes that one must not generalize about people, that one must always be sensitive to that which is real. Arthur Hannah gave her the first job in radio in the serial *Nora Drake*.

Ruby knew before she finished college that, for better or for worse, the theater was going to claim her. Upon graduation from Hunter as a language major she took a job as a translator in an export house. She also painted buttons in a factory and distributed soap samples in rancid Harlem tenements before getting her first Broadway role in *Jeb*. The year was 1946.

Playwright Robert Audrey had written *Jeb,* the story of a black veteran of World War II, and Herman Shumlin had decided to put it on Broadway. Ruby left her job at the export house to take the understudy role of Libby. She was so effective she eventually won the role. Meanwhile, she was taking particular notice of the tall handsome young man playing Jeb.

His name was Ossie Davis and he wasn't at all like what the picture she had seen of him in the papers suggested. Ruby had looked at that picture before meeting Ossie and had decided the casting director had gone down south and snatched a yokel from behind a mule and plow for the role of Jeb. It would be *just like* white folks, she thought, to cast somebody in the role who had never in his life had an acting lesson! Why on earth, she wondered, hadn't they selected someone from the American Negro Theatre?

Ruby Dee couldn't have been more wrong. Ossie Davis was from the south but had never in his life been on a farm. He had gone to college, and he had been working for a long time with Dick Campbell and the Rose Mc-Clendon Players. Moreover, he had a wealth of theater experience, including writing, and he was still a very young man. Ruby was quite abashed that she had mis-judged Ossie so badly and as he worked she became completely fascinated by what she saw and, more important, what she felt.

"It was during this period that I had the strangest experience in my life," she reminisces. "It's a feeling I've never had since. Ossie was tying his necktie in one of the scenes and it was as if an electric charge passed through me—this feeling that I would have some connection with him. It was the closest thing I have ever had to a supernatural experience."

Though critical reviews of *Jeb* were better than good, it ran for no more than seven performances. But Ruby and Ossie had become close friends. They worked together again in the road company of the Broadway smash hit *Anna Lucasta*. And they were together in a dreadful flop. When that one closed Ossie borrowed ten dollars from his brother so he and Ruby could be married. The newlyweds settled in a modest flat and, with fingers crossed, began what Ruby calls "a strange life together in the Bronx."

By this time Ruby had been exposed to the prodigious talents of some of the older black artists who had never received their due share of recognition. She was particularly moved by the performance of veteran Abbie Mitchell with whom she was privileged to work in a production of *Arsenic and Old Lace*. And there were Laura Bowman, Evelyn Ellis, and Edna Thomas, all inspired by the incomparable Rose McClendon. All of them, Ruby sadly knew, had never *begun* to have the exposure enjoyed by Helen Hayes, Bette Davis, and Katherine Hepburn. She, herself, was not getting, as a young actress, the kind of acting experience so necessary, if one is to become craftworthy.

The gnawing and agonizing truth of the paucity of opportunities for black performers impelled Ruby to join forces with Frederick O'Neal, Charles Gordone, her husband, Ossie, and others to form the Coordinating Council for Negro Performers. Their purpose was to induce those who control the entertainment industry to increase the level of participation of black performers in the theater, films, and television. Her own personal feeling of being "always behind" white performers who work regularly spurred Ruby forward. It also sharpened her growing empathy with others who were denied and rejected and it led her, along with her husband, into the front ranks of the civil rights movement.

Ruby's empathy with the downtrodden first exhibited itself publicly when she was not more than eleven years old. A music teacher of whom she was fond had lost her job in a curtailment move directed at the Federal Music Program. Those were pre-World War II days and jobs were scarce. The dismissed teacher, terrified and distraught, committed suicide. A Harlem mass meeting followed the tragedy, with Adam Clayton Powell its principal speaker. And little Ruby Wallace was called upon to speak—on behalf of her deceased teacher—for a restoration of the curtailed music program.

Her second involvement in civil rights activity occurred when, in 1953, Julius and Ethel Rosenberg were about to be executed at Sing Sing prison for conspiring to commit wartime sabotage. Ruby, then a rising actress, with three Hollywood films to her credit, was concerned for the Rosenbergs' children. She felt compelled to join others who were vocally opposed to the hard-line stand of the U. S. Government. She spoke out against the impending executions and the press quickly sought her out for interviews. Kindly reporters avowed she was being "exploited by Communists." Those not so kindly accused her of being a Communist sympathizer—if not a card-carrying Party member.

But the barbs were matched by bouquets from sources sympathetic to the Rosenbergs. For the first time Ruby

Dee was given a non-Negro part in a play. She appeared as the Defending Angel in *The World of Sholem Aleichem,* directed and produced by Howard De Silva and Arnold Ford and presented at New York's Barbizon Plaza Theatre.

"There," she recalls, "I met many people whose whole lives were wrapped up in the theater. And *then* I began to sense everything I didn't know about acting. It was the springboard from which I saw the blending of art and life; and suddenly I realized that *all the things happening to black people* are not exclusive!"

Ossie Davis shared his wife's sentiments to the extent that his own *Purlie Victorious,* which was to become a Broadway hit nearly a decade later, was greatly influenced by *The World of Sholem Aleichem.* Both Ossie and Ruby had been convinced of and inspired by the importance of the interrelatedness of human cultures.

It was shortly before her appearances in *Sholem Aleichem* that Ruby's first motion picture was seen on the screens of the nation's movie houses. Its title was *No Way Out* and it was a story of a young hospital staff doctor accused of causing the death of a patient. The doctor was played by Sidney Poiter. His patient was white.

Ruby's feeling about *No Way Out* is that for its time (1950) it was a revolutionary film in that for the first time on the American screen blacks and whites confronted each other in a very real way. The violence of the film's riot scene involved her in a way she felt she as an artist must be involved if she is to say anything of significance.

Ruby Dee appeared in subsequent films, notably, *Take a Giant Step* (1958), *A Raisin in the Sun* (1960), and *Gone Are the Days* (1963), a film version of *Purlie Victorious.* On the stage she had played the role of Ruth Younger in Lorraine Hansberry's great play, *A Raisin in the Sun,* and of the beguiling Lutiebelle in Ossie's *Purlie Victorious.* Even in the comic aspects of Purlie, she was ever conscious of violence—the emotional violence involved in being black in a white racist setting.

But a very real violence was to involve her in another way in the autumn of 1963. Addie May Collins, Carol Robertson, Cynthia Dianne Wesley, and Carol Denise McNair lived in Birmingham, Alabama. They were black children. Carol Wesley, the youngest, was eleven. The others were fourteen. As they sat in their Sunday School class on September 12, 1963, a hate bomb which they never heard exploded in their Sixteenth Street Baptist Church. No one was then, nor has been since, apprehended for the crime.

News of the brutal murders of the children horrified and enraged decent Americans. In New York City a group of black artists headed by writers James Baldwin and John Oliver Killens, with the latter's wife, Grace, and folk singer Odetta joined Ruby and Ossie Davis in forming the Association of Artists for Freedom. The group also included attorney Clarence Jones, actor Godfrey Cambridge, writer Paule Marshall and painter Ernest Crichlow. Their purpose was to organize a nationwide boycott against the customary rash of lavish and frivolous Christmas spending in view of the nature of the atrocity at Birmingham. Their campaign did curb such spending, particularly in black communities where many residents used their Christmas money to support various civil rights groups.

Meanwhile Ossie and Ruby Davis together lent their talents to assist many of the civil rights leaders. They were with the Kings during the March on Washington and they worked with Bayard Rustin and A. Philip Randolph. The fact that Ruby's father, Marshall Wallace, had been a railroad man prior to Mr. Randolph's organizing of the Pullman car porters, made her personally conscious of that respected organizer's contribution to labor. The Davises have appeared on panels with Dr. Kenneth B. Clark and with Mrs. Fannie Lou Hamer. And it is significant that the National Urban League under Whitney Young's directorship has seen fit to award them the League's Frederick Douglass Award for 1970. The medallion is presented annually to New York Community leaders for distinguished leadership toward equal opportunity.

Ruby Dee does not separate her art from other aspects of her life. She sees her function as an artist in terms of the relevancy of what she performs to the needs of those for whom she performs. For instance, while she has reservations about some aspects of her latest film, *Uptight* (1968) she has this to say:

"I feel strongly about *Uptight*. It's not as clean as I would like to have seen it but it was an effort. It sought to define the thinking of black people and I found that challenging and rewarding in terms of the militants and the nationalists who have given up on the system."

It gives her concern that Hollywood's doors are not open to books written by black writers. Both she and Ossie feel strongly that the best works of John O. Killens, Margaret Walker, and Paule Marshall, to mention but three, are worthy of serious consideration by the film capital's decision-makers.

"I'm eager to see, before I die, that some of our major writers get major treatment in terms of films," she quietly asserts.

Between engagements Ruby Dee is working on a poetry anthology for junior high school youngsters. Her experiences in touring colleges leads her to the conclusion that the things young people's theater groups do need to be more "relevant." She also believes that young people of this nation need to become better acquainted with black writers and what their works are really all about.

Young people are very real to Ruby, since she and Ossie

have three of their own. Their eldest, Nora, is a Vassar
College student. Guy, the next, was recently arrested with
his father in an antiwar demonstration in New Rochelle,
New York. Each of the three young Davises has had a
taste of the life of the theater, but it is LaVerne, the
youngest, described by her mother as "mentally and spirit-
ually solid," who leans quite decidedly in the direction of
the theater. But Ruby doesn't push. She is grateful that
each of her young people is concentrating upon other
areas of possible vocational activity—just in case.

In speaking of her civil rights activities Ruby's words
return easily and naturally to Malcolm X:

"He came to Ossie's play, *Purlie Victorious,* and we invited him to our house. He later told my brother that he
deeply appreciated our knowing his beliefs by not per-
mitting anyone to smoke or drink while he was our guest."

Like many artists, the Davises are not joiners. They had
no wish to become Muslims, but they were admiring of
Malcolm's efforts to instill a sense of morality and pride
in black men. Their friendship with the militant leader
was sincere enough to permit them to see Malcolm's weaknesses along with his strengths.

The Davises were fully aware of the disparaging things
Malcolm had publicly said about other black leaders. So
it was the more significant when Malcolm said privately
to them:

"If they (Roy Wilkins, King, and Whitney Young) had
any sense they could make good use of us Muslims. They
could say to the power boys, 'look at me. I'm a nice guy.
You don't want to deal with those alley cats back there.' "

Ruby sensed early that Malcolm saw himself as a symbol of something the peacemakers among black leadership
could use as a threat in order to make their own gains. It
was this perception that prompted her and Ossie to ar-
range a private meeting near New York City.

Dr. King, unable to attend because of a previous engagement, sent a representative. Juanita (Mrs. Sidney) Poiter, Whitney Young, and the Davises joined Malcolm in a meeting of mutual understanding. During the session Whitney Young tried to pin Malcolm down to a specific program. Would it be an effort to eliminate slums? If so, why not organize a committee whose job it would be to concentrate on housing.

"We came to realize," Ruby recalls, "that Malcolm was a religionist and a philosopher rather than an organizer. Even the pulling together of the Organization Of African Unity was too specific a task for him. He needed to *inspire* it and to leave other people to do the organizing."

There was the day that Malcolm wanted to meet Paul Robeson and Davis arranged it.

"Suppose he had not been denied these people in his childhood?" Ruby suggests. "What a difference that might have been."

The afternoon sun begins to fill the spacious porch and Ruby Dee smiles slowly and thoughtfully. "But then," she adds, "aren't we all striving for the same goals?"

Index

237

Index

Index